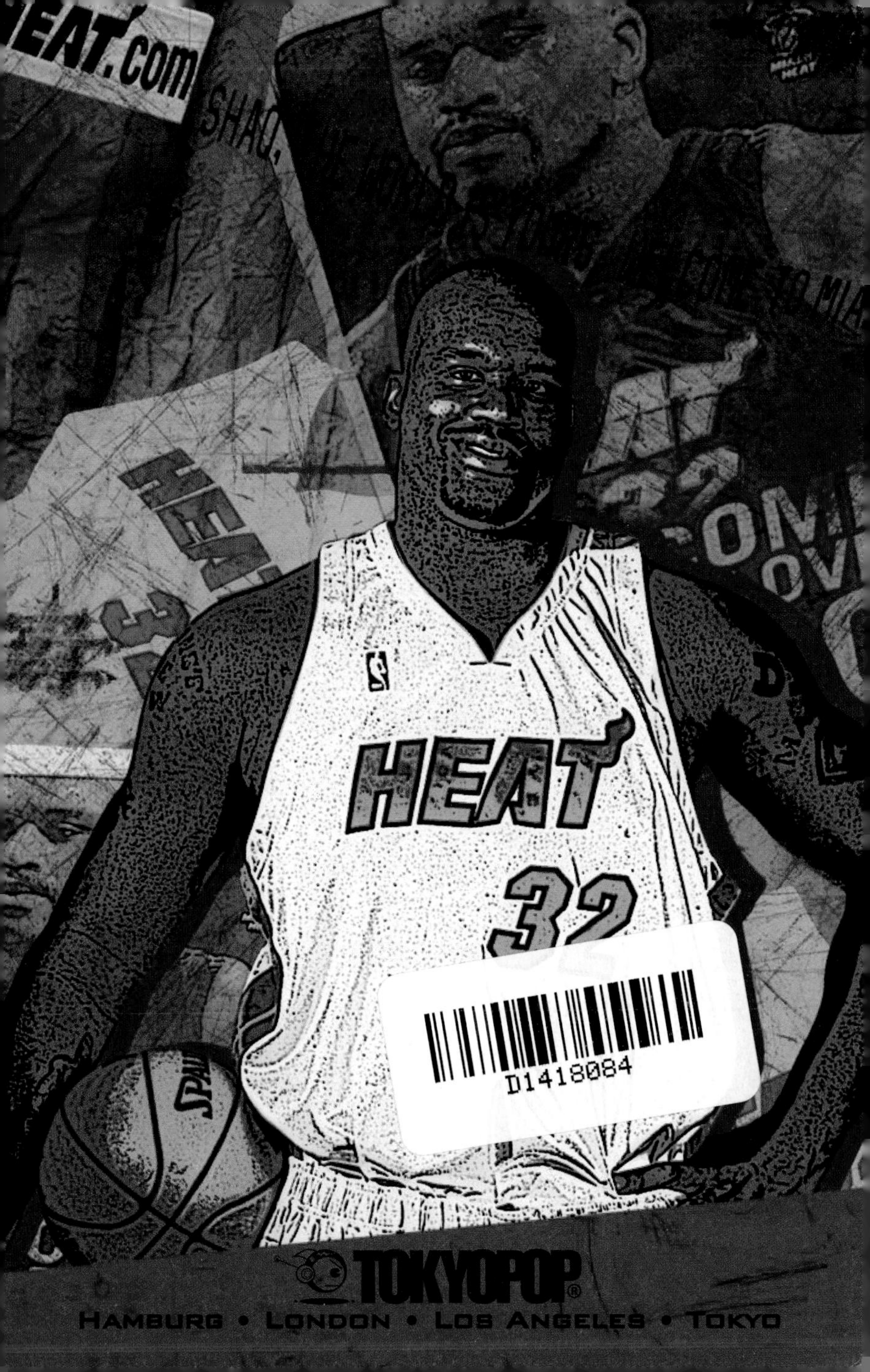
HEAT.com
SHAQ.
HEAT
32

TOKYOPOP®
HAMBURG • LONDON • LOS ANGELES • TOKYO

Contributing Editor - John Fawaz
Graphic Design and Lettering - Jennifer Nunn-Iwai,
Monalisa de Asis, Tomás Montalvo-Lagos
Cover Layout - Jennifer Nunn-Iwai
Character Design - Tomás Montalvo-Lagos
Illustrations - Michael Paolilli and Tomás Montalvo-Lagos

Editor - Jod Kaftan
Senior Designer - Suzanna Lakatos
Digital Imaging Manager - Chris Buford
Pre-Press Manager - Antonio DePietro
Production Managers - Jennifer Miller and Mutsumi Miyazaki
Art Director - Matt Alford
Senior Editor - Elizabeth Hurchalla
Managing Editor - Jill Freshney
VP of Production - Ron Klamert
President & C.O.O. - John Parker
Publisher & C.E.O. - Stuart Levy

E-mail: info@tokyopop.com

A **TOKYOPOP**® Cine-Manga® book

TOKYOPOP Inc.
5900 Wilshire Blvd., Suite 2000
Los Angeles, CA 90036

GREATEST STARS OF THE NBA: SHAQUILLE O'NEAL

TOKYOPOP special thanks: John Hareas and Michael Levine of the NBA

Additional material ©2004 TOKYOPOP Inc. All rights reserved.

ISBN: 159532-181-0
First TOKYOPOP® printing: November 2004

10 9 8 7 6 5 4 3 2 1

Printed in the United States of America

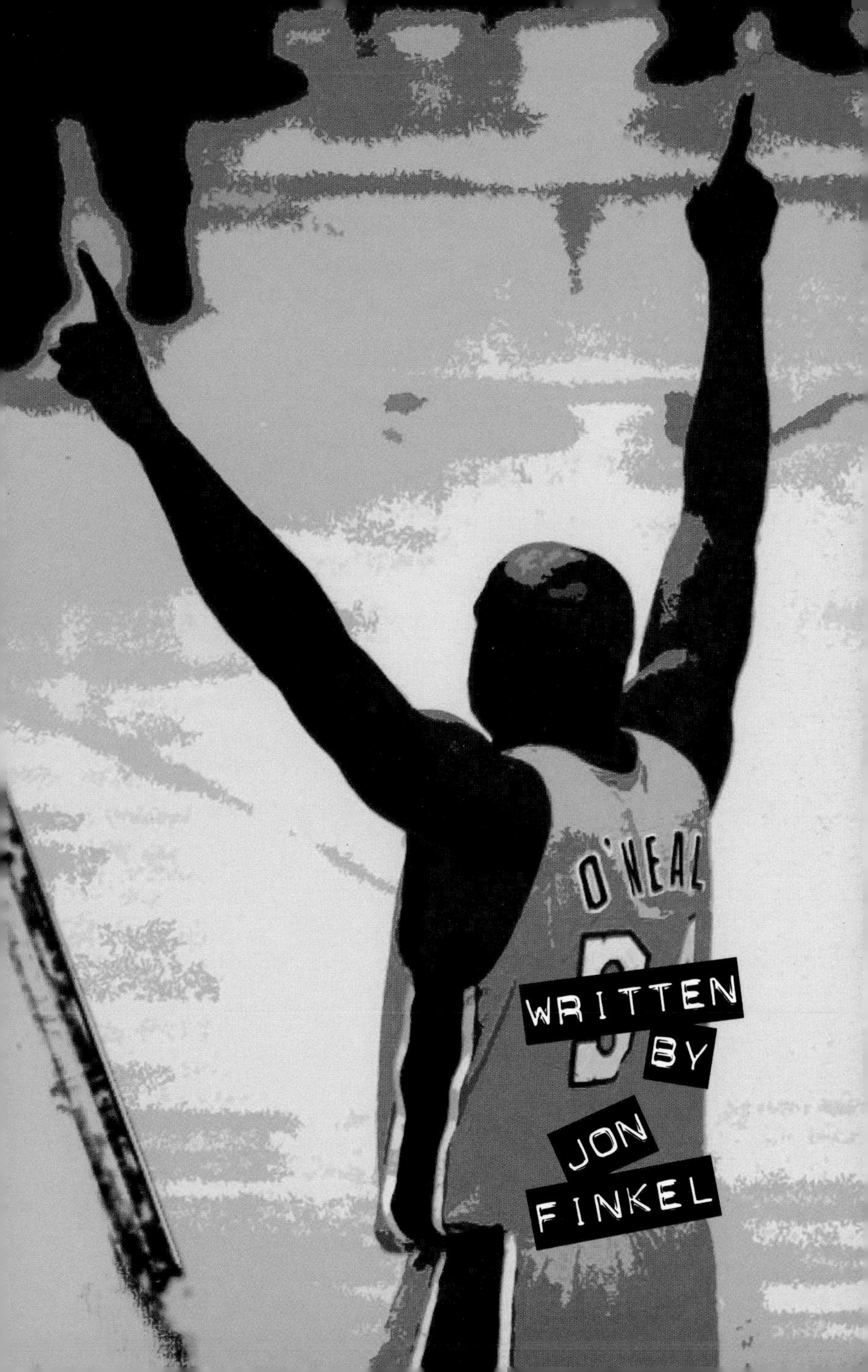
O'NEAL
WRITTEN BY
JON FINKEL

CONTENTS//:

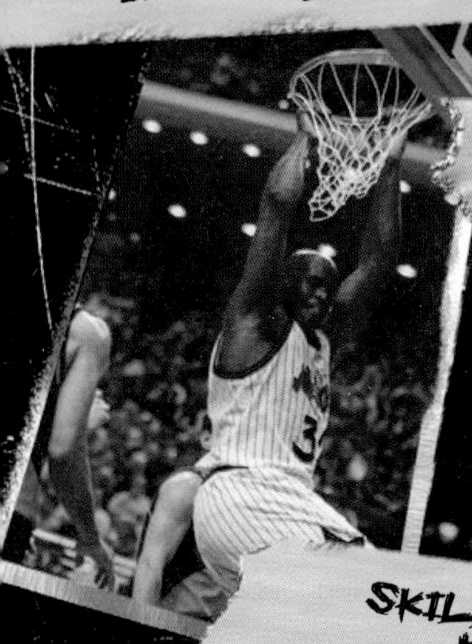

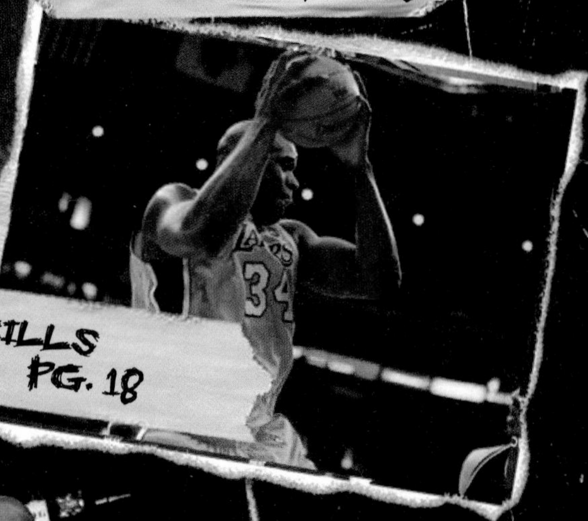

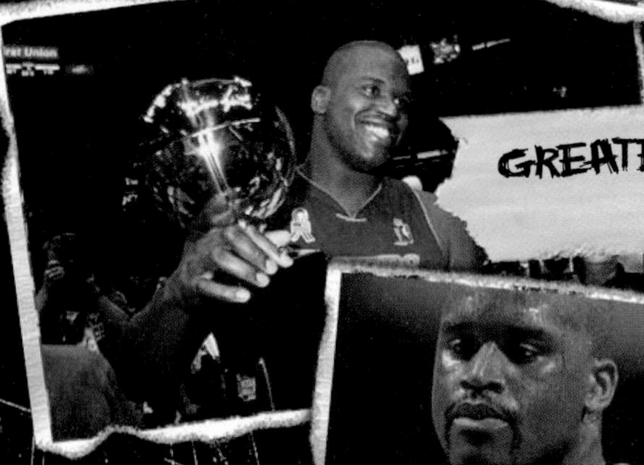

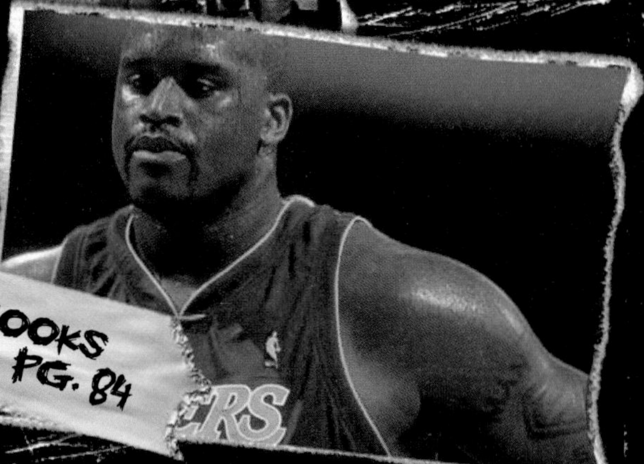

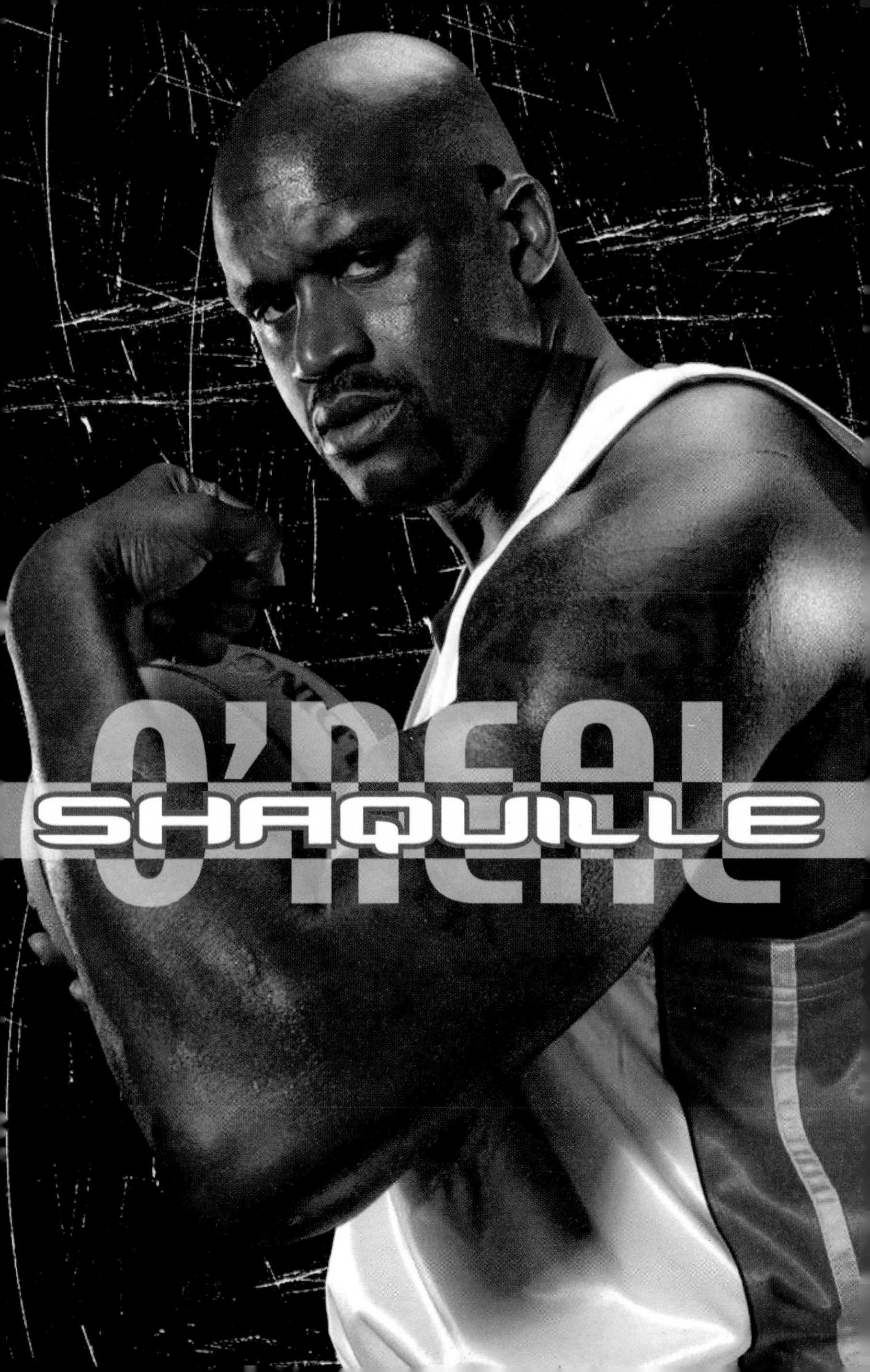
O'NEAL
SHAQUILLE

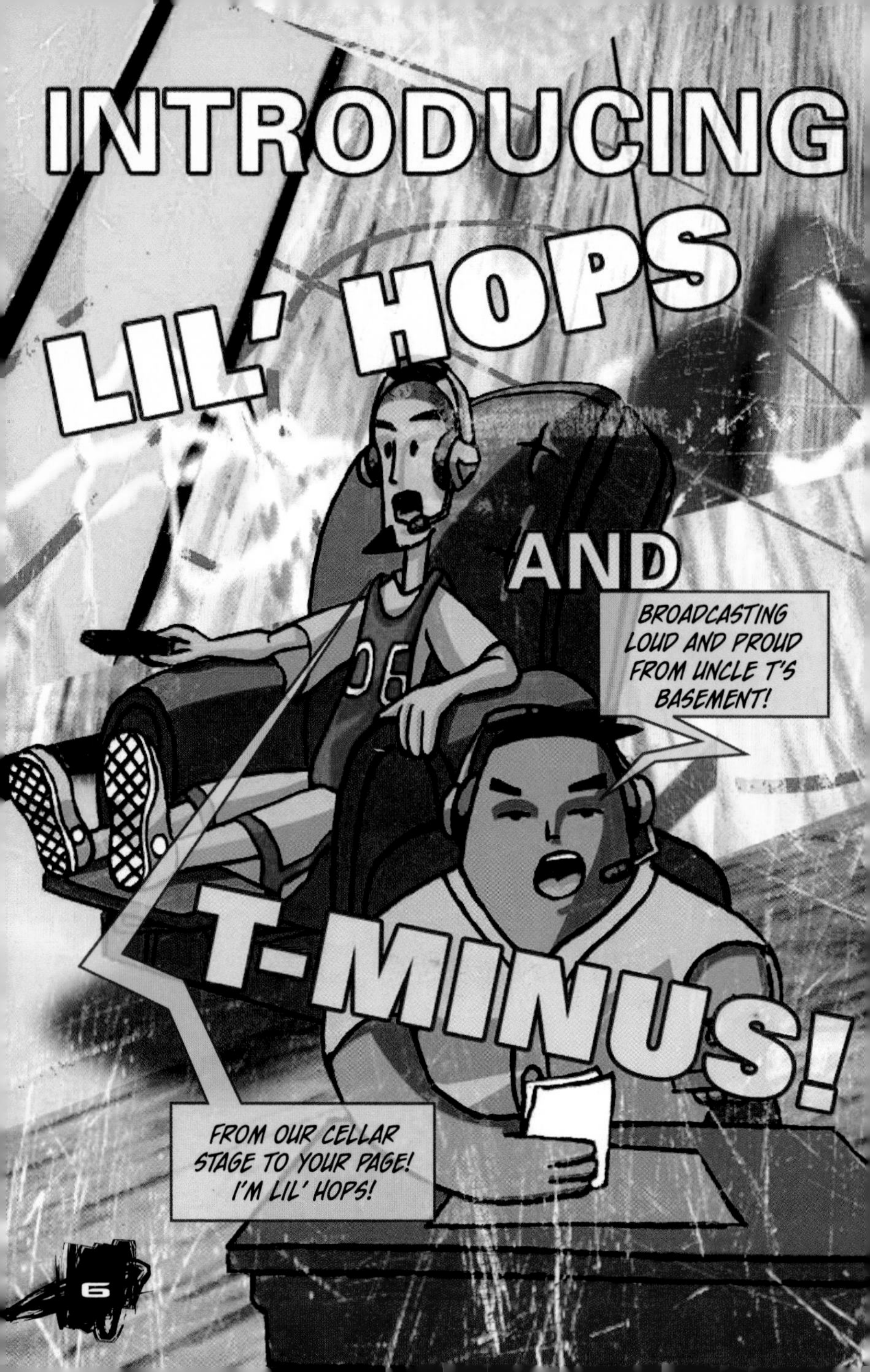
INTRODUCING
LIL' HOPS
AND
BROADCASTING LOUD AND PROUD FROM UNCLE T'S BASEMENT!
T-MINUS!
FROM OUR CELLAR STAGE TO YOUR PAGE! I'M LIL' HOPS!

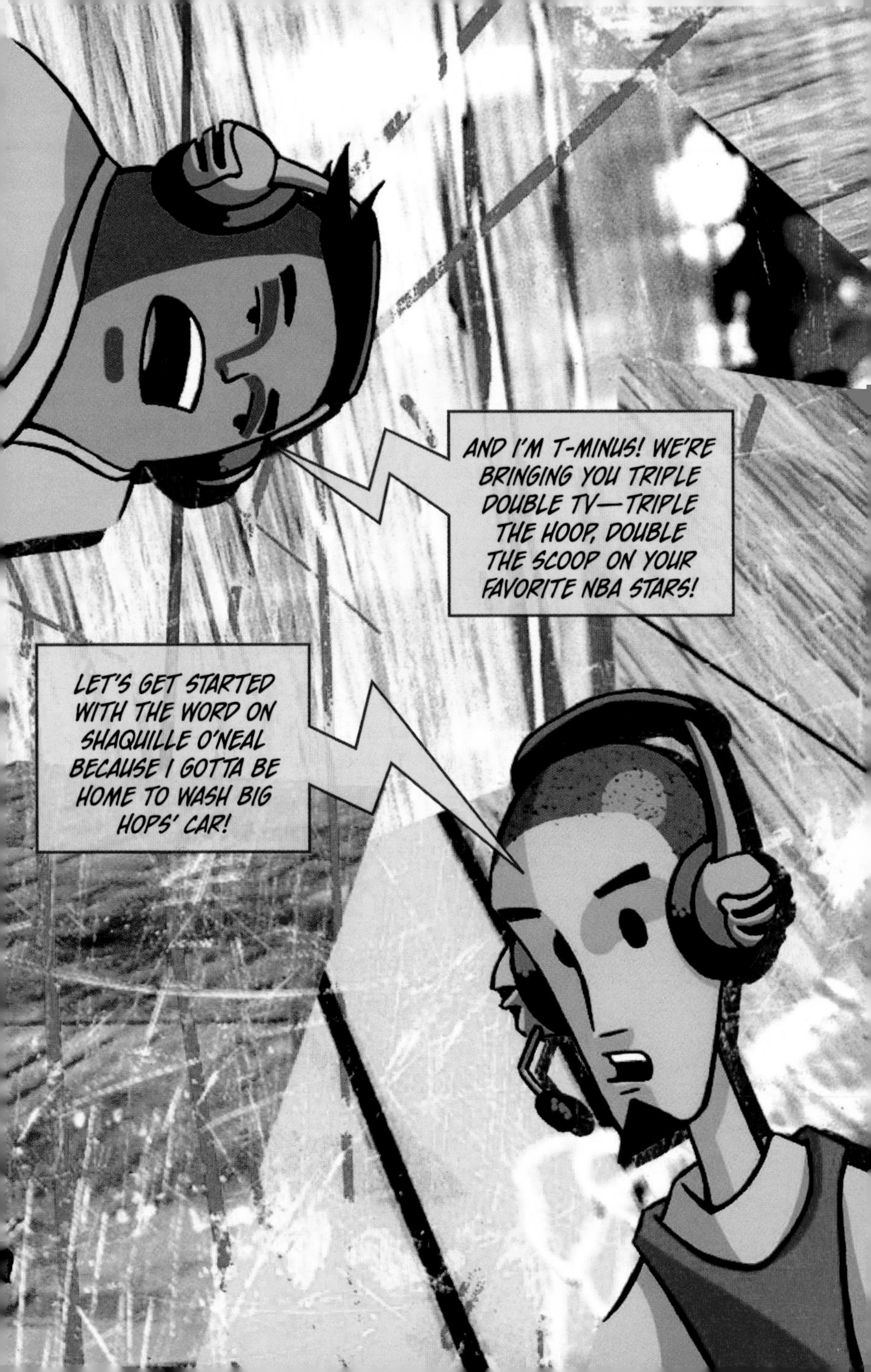
AND I'M T-MINUS! WE'RE BRINGING YOU TRIPLE DOUBLE TV—TRIPLE THE HOOP, DOUBLE THE SCOOP ON YOUR FAVORITE NBA STARS!
LET'S GET STARTED WITH THE WORD ON SHAQUILLE O'NEAL BECAUSE I GOTTA BE HOME TO WASH BIG HOPS' CAR!

A STAR IS BORN

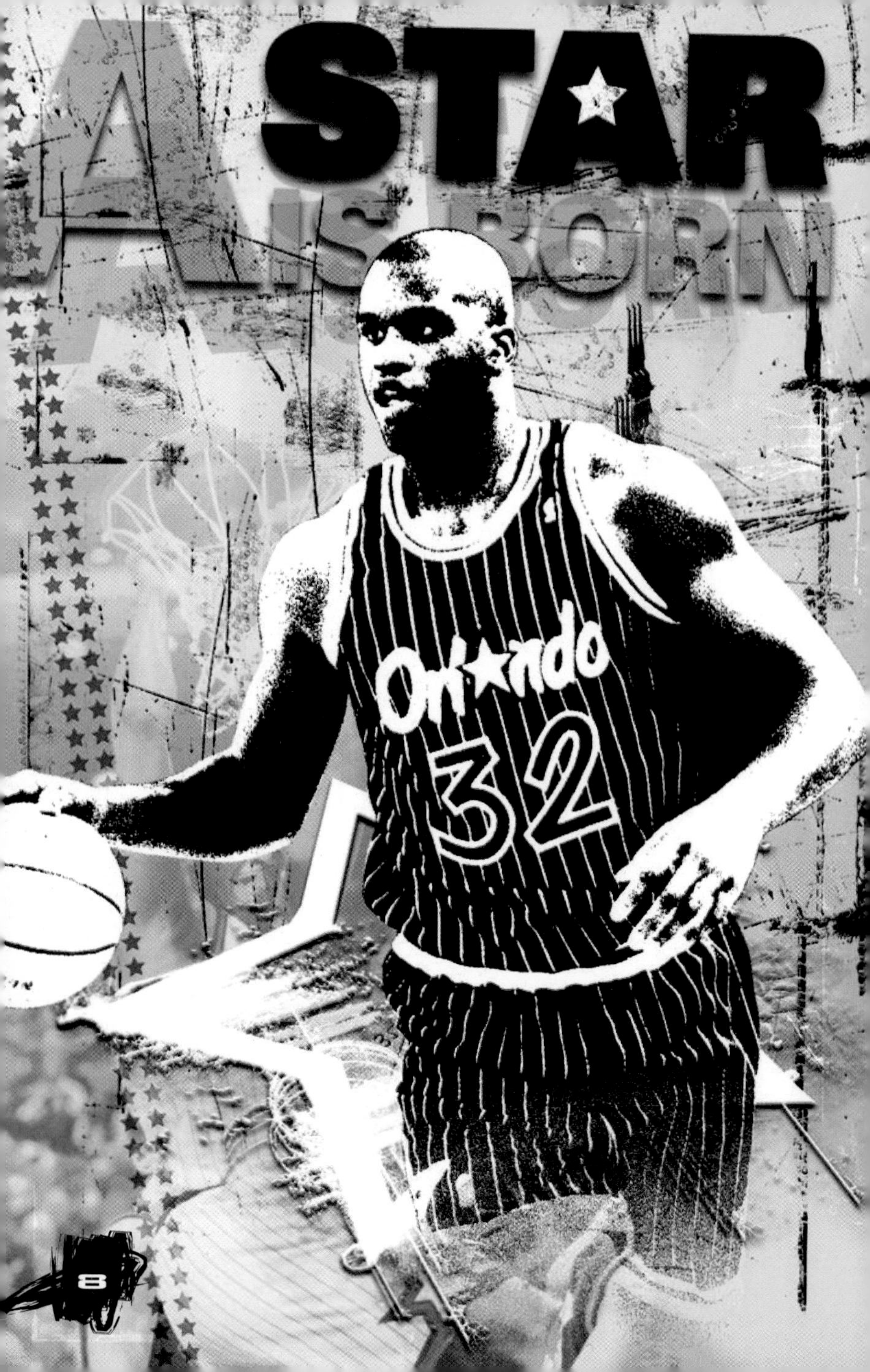
Orlando
32

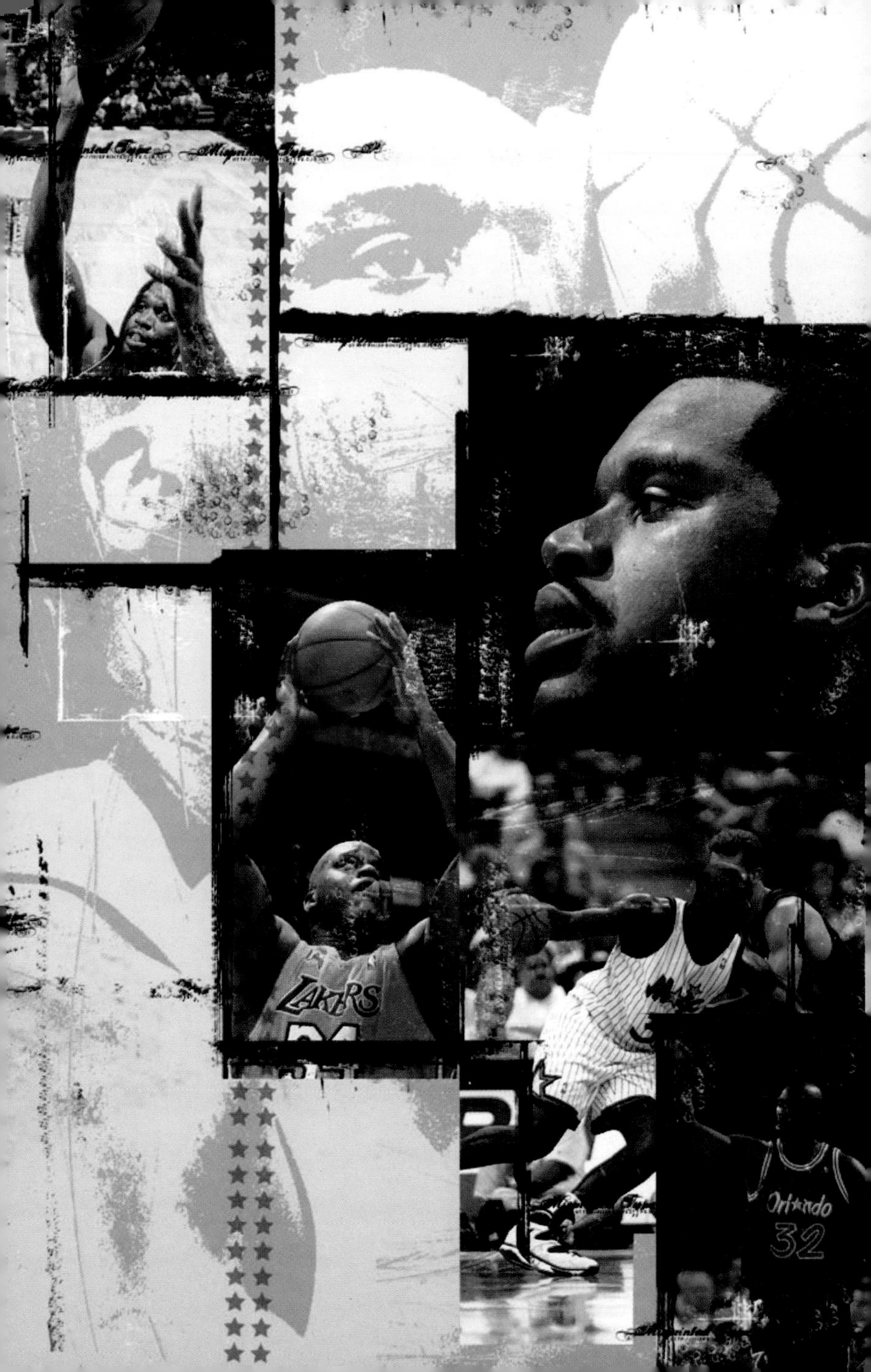
LAKERS
Orlando
32

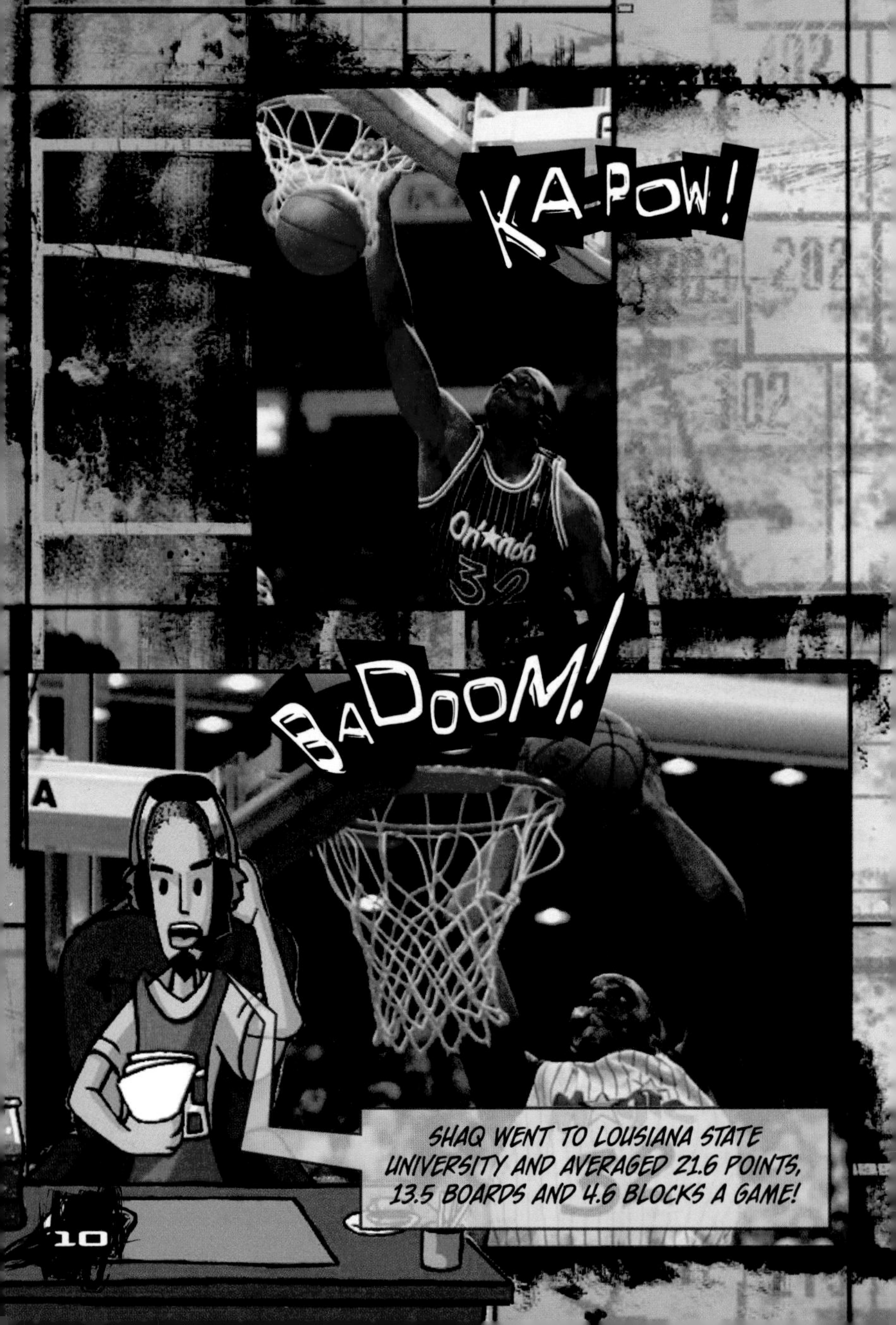
KA-POW!
BADOOM!
SHAQ WENT TO LOUSIANA STATE UNIVERSITY AND AVERAGED 21.6 POINTS, 13.5 BOARDS AND 4.6 BLOCKS A GAME!

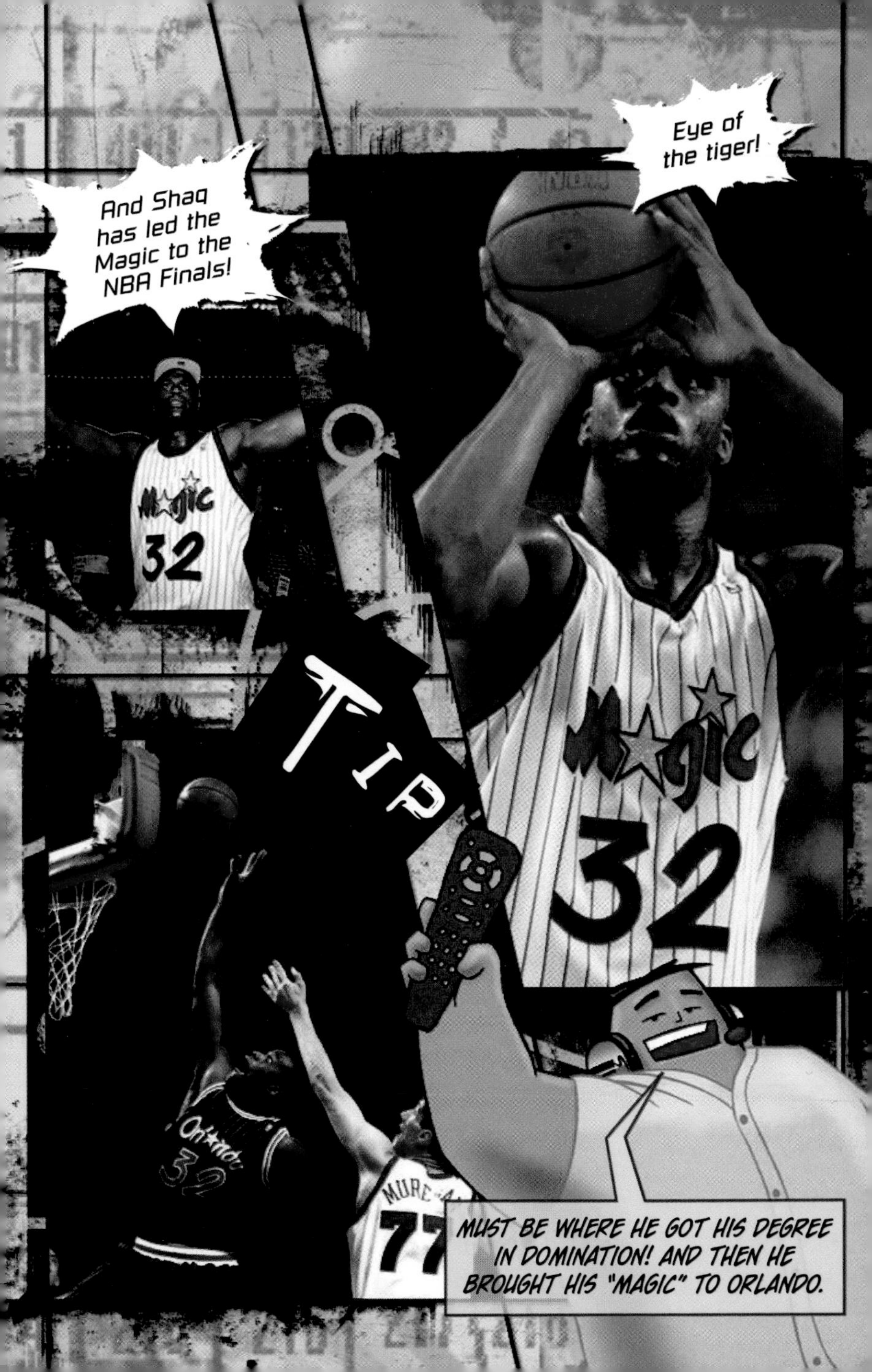
And Shaq has led the Magic to the NBA Finals!
Eye of the tiger!
TIP
MUST BE WHERE HE GOT HIS DEGREE IN DOMINATION! AND THEN HE BROUGHT HIS "MAGIC" TO ORLANDO.

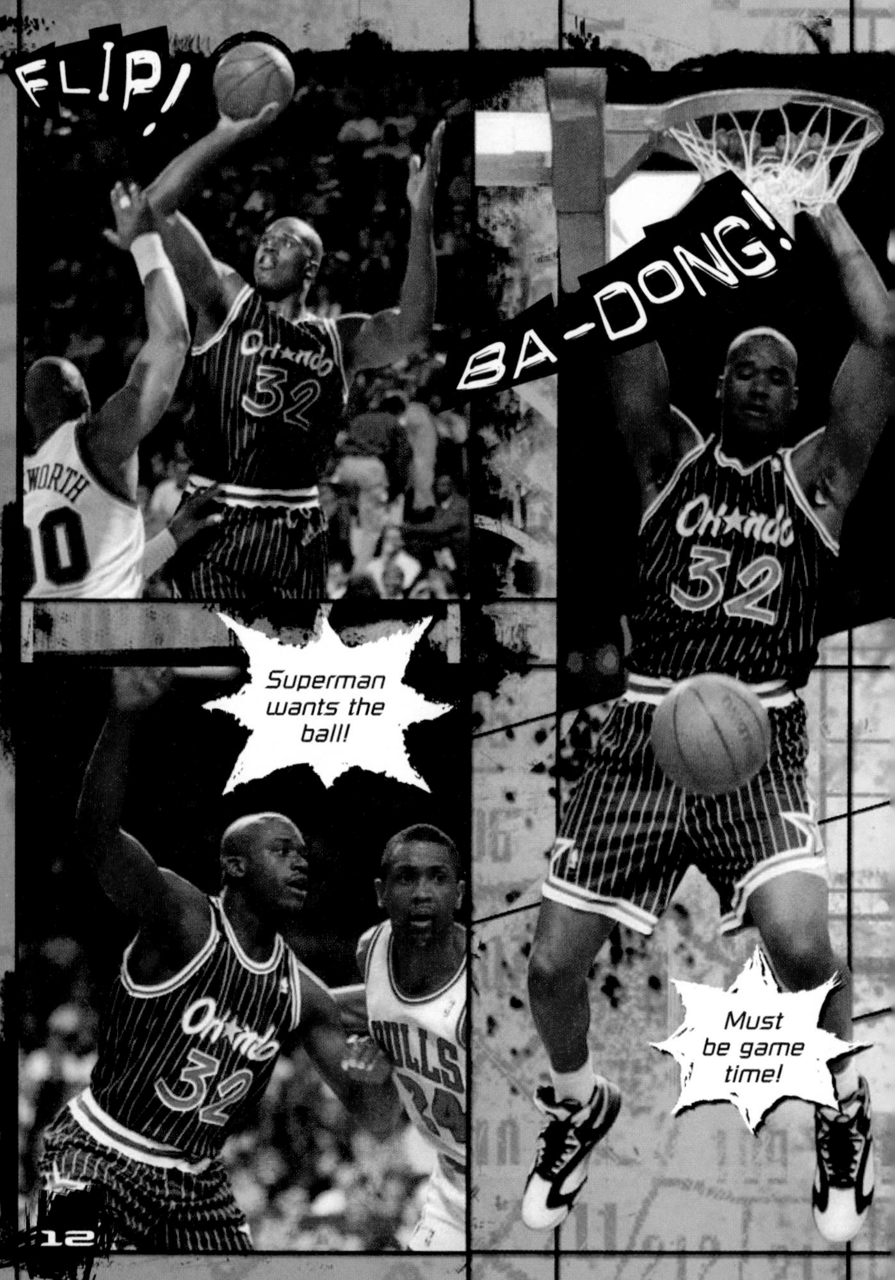
FLIP!
Superman wants the ball!
BA-DONG!
Must be game time!

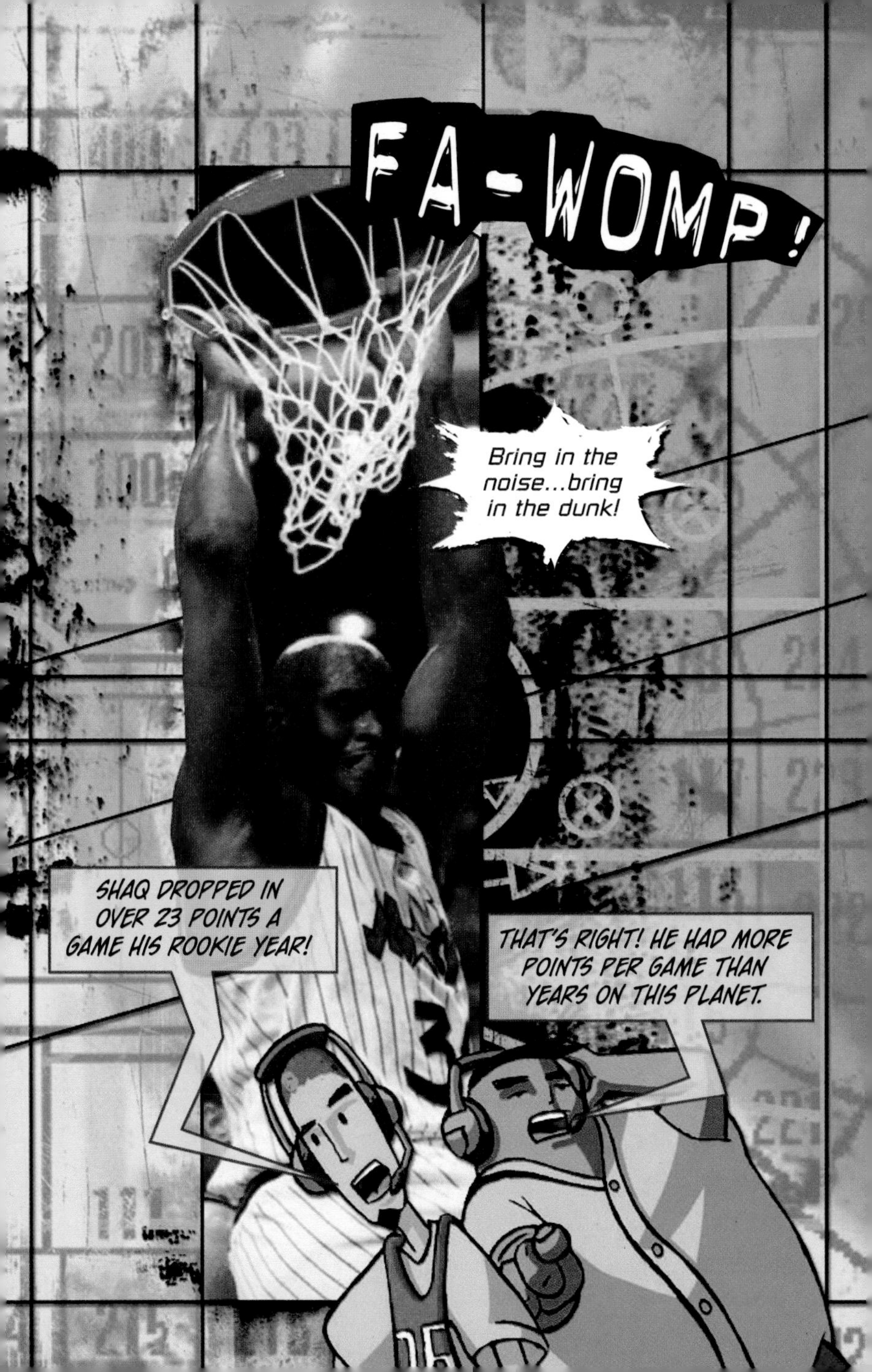
FA-WOMP!
Bring in the noise...bring in the dunk!
SHAQ DROPPED IN OVER 23 POINTS A GAME HIS ROOKIE YEAR!
THAT'S RIGHT! HE HAD MORE POINTS PER GAME THAN YEARS ON THIS PLANET.

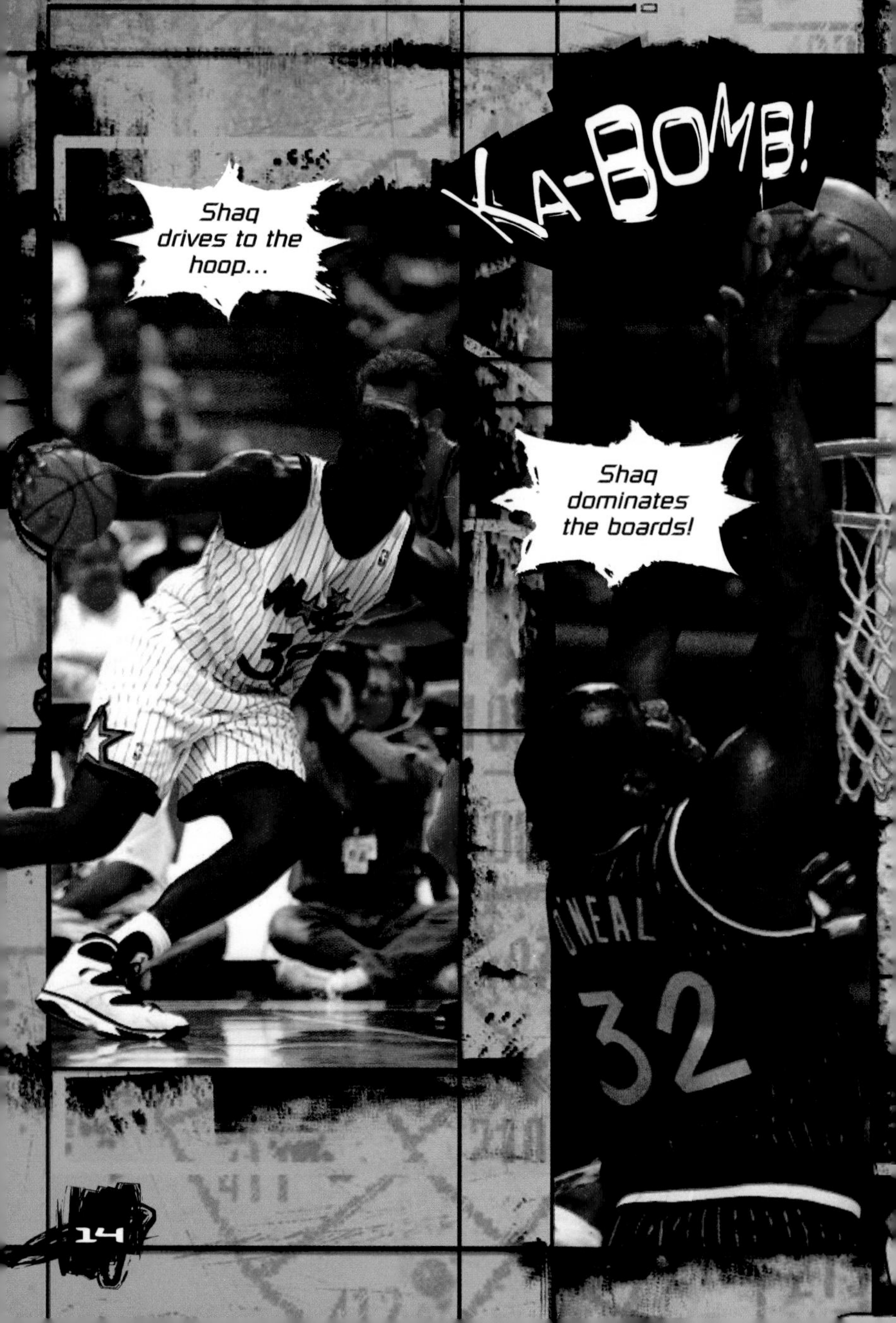
Shaq drives to the hoop...
KA-BOMB!
Shaq dominates the boards!
ONEAL
32

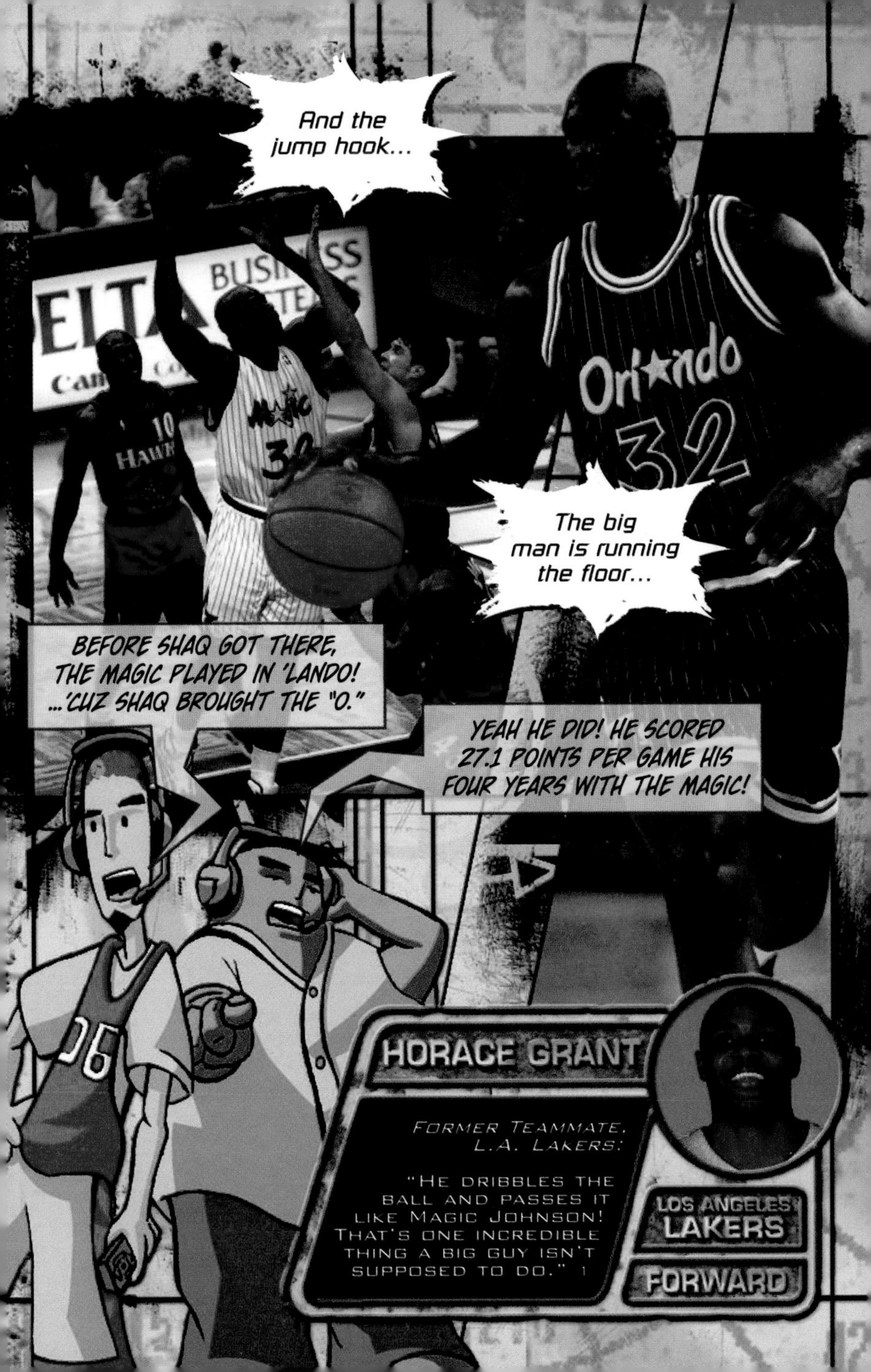
And the jump hook...
The big man is running the floor...
BEFORE SHAQ GOT THERE, THE MAGIC PLAYED IN 'LANDO! ...'CUZ SHAQ BROUGHT THE "O."
YEAH HE DID! HE SCORED 27.1 POINTS PER GAME HIS FOUR YEARS WITH THE MAGIC!
HORACE GRANT
FORMER TEAMMATE, L.A. LAKERS:
"HE DRIBBLES THE BALL AND PASSES IT LIKE MAGIC JOHNSON! THAT'S ONE INCREDIBLE THING A BIG GUY ISN'T SUPPOSED TO DO." 1
LOS ANGELES LAKERS
FORWARD

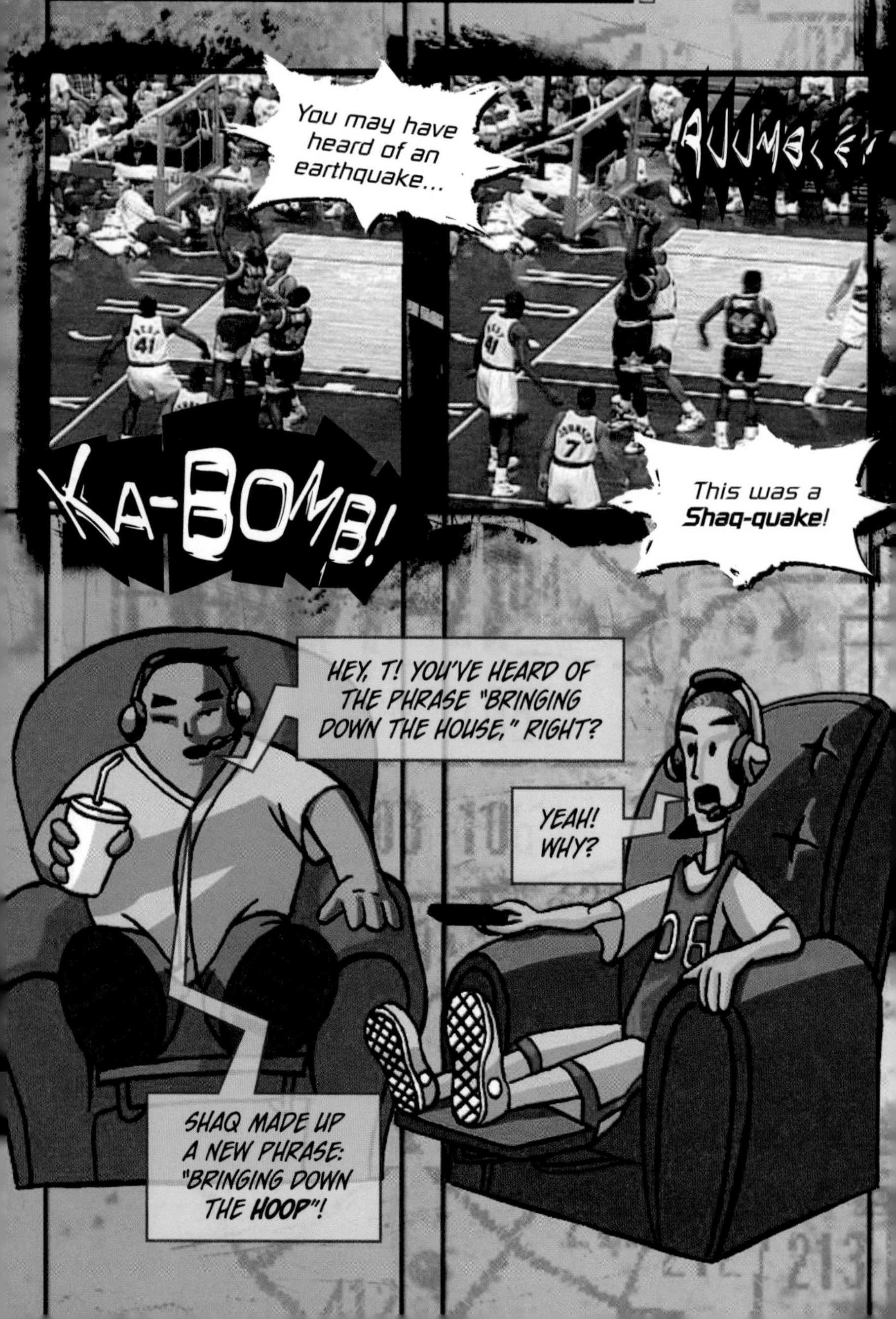
You may have heard of an earthquake...
KA-BOMB!
RUUMBLE!
This was a **Shaq-quake**!
HEY, T! YOU'VE HEARD OF THE PHRASE "BRINGING DOWN THE HOUSE," RIGHT?
YEAH! WHY?
SHAQ MADE UP A NEW PHRASE: "BRINGING DOWN THE **HOOP**"!

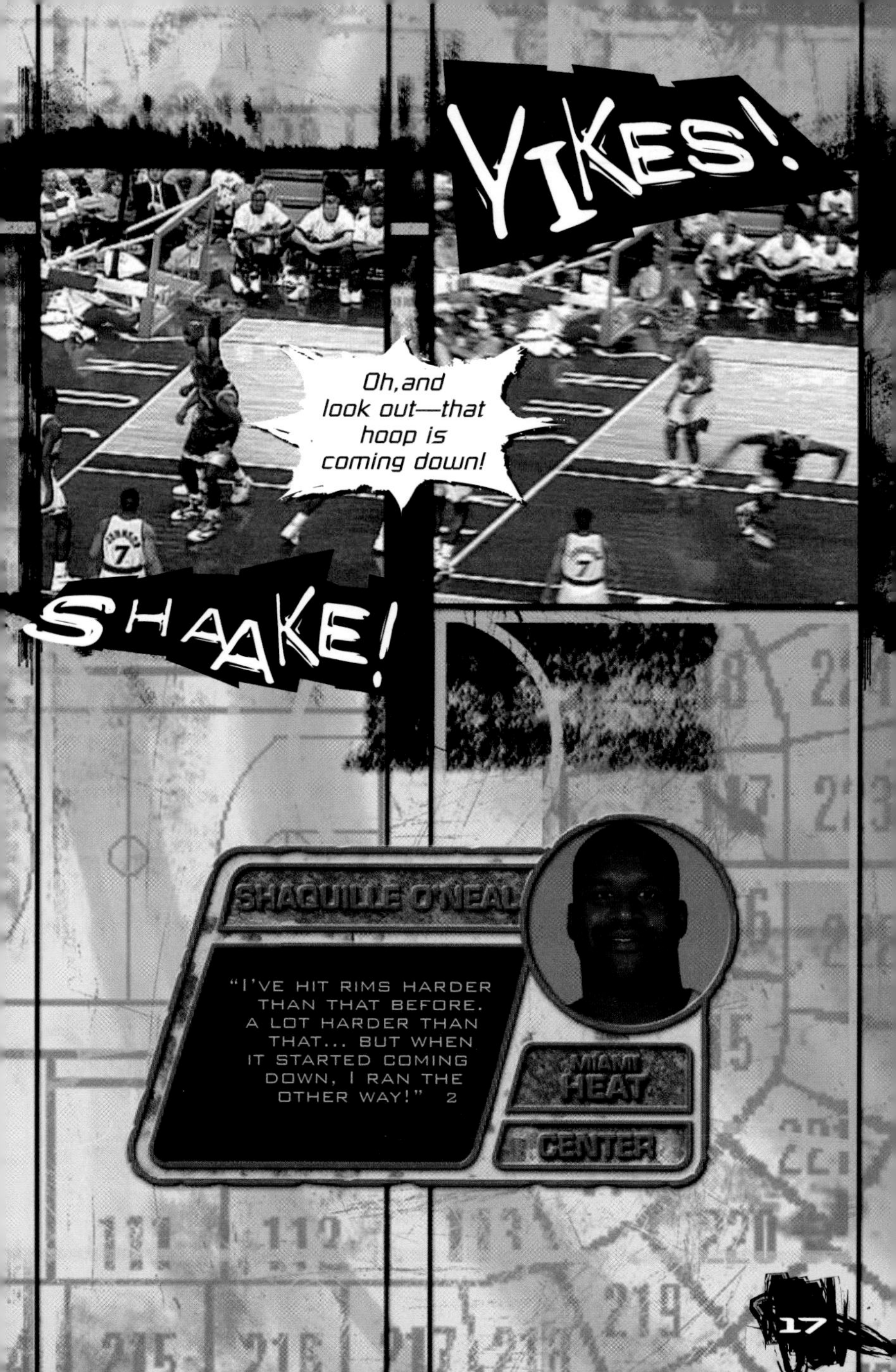
YIKES!
Oh, and look out—that hoop is coming down!
SHAAKE!
SHAQUILLE O'NEAL
"I'VE HIT RIMS HARDER THAN THAT BEFORE. A LOT HARDER THAN THAT... BUT WHEN IT STARTED COMING DOWN, I RAN THE OTHER WAY!" 2
MIAMI HEAT
CENTER

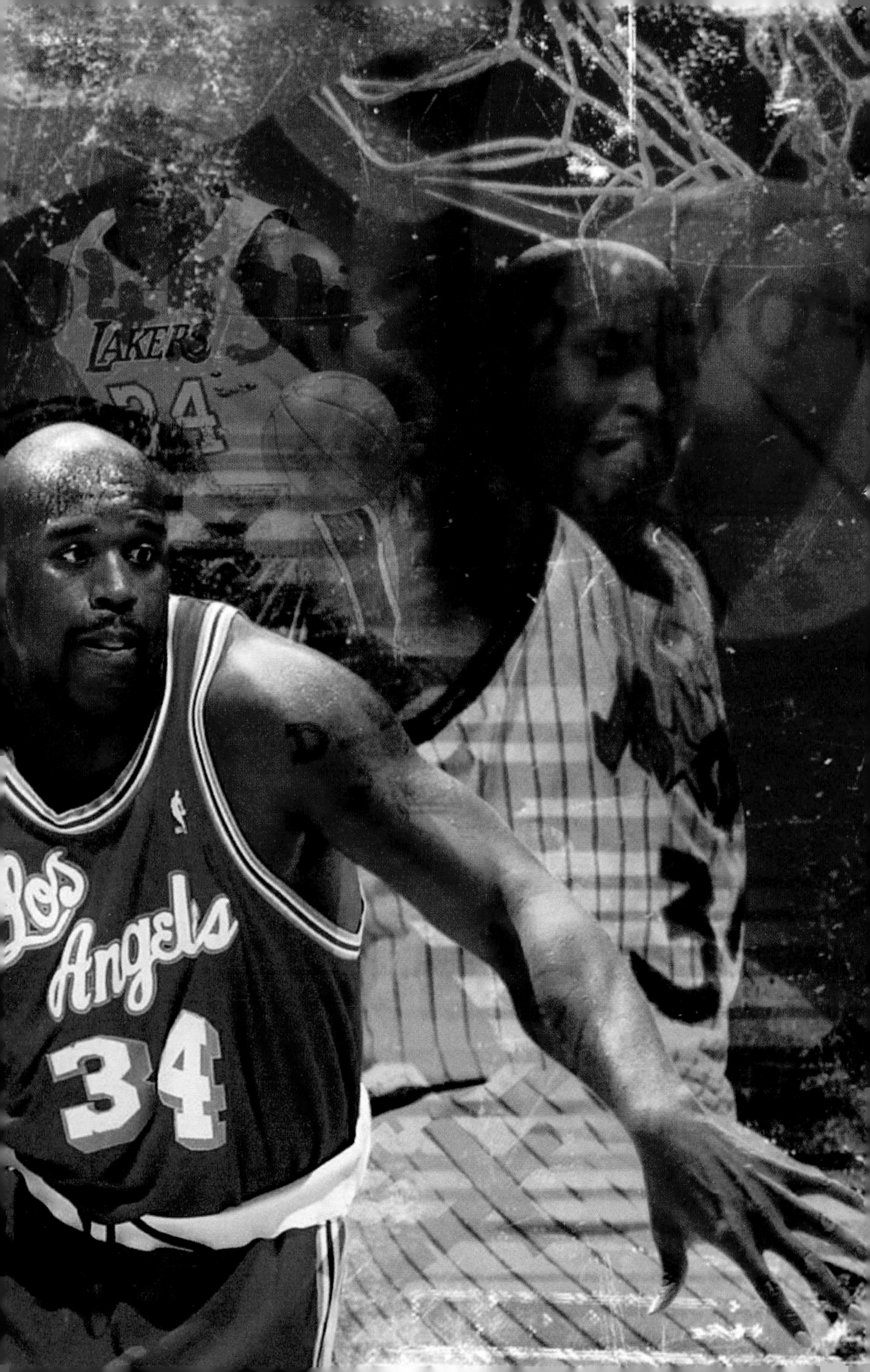
LAKERS
34
34

SKILLS

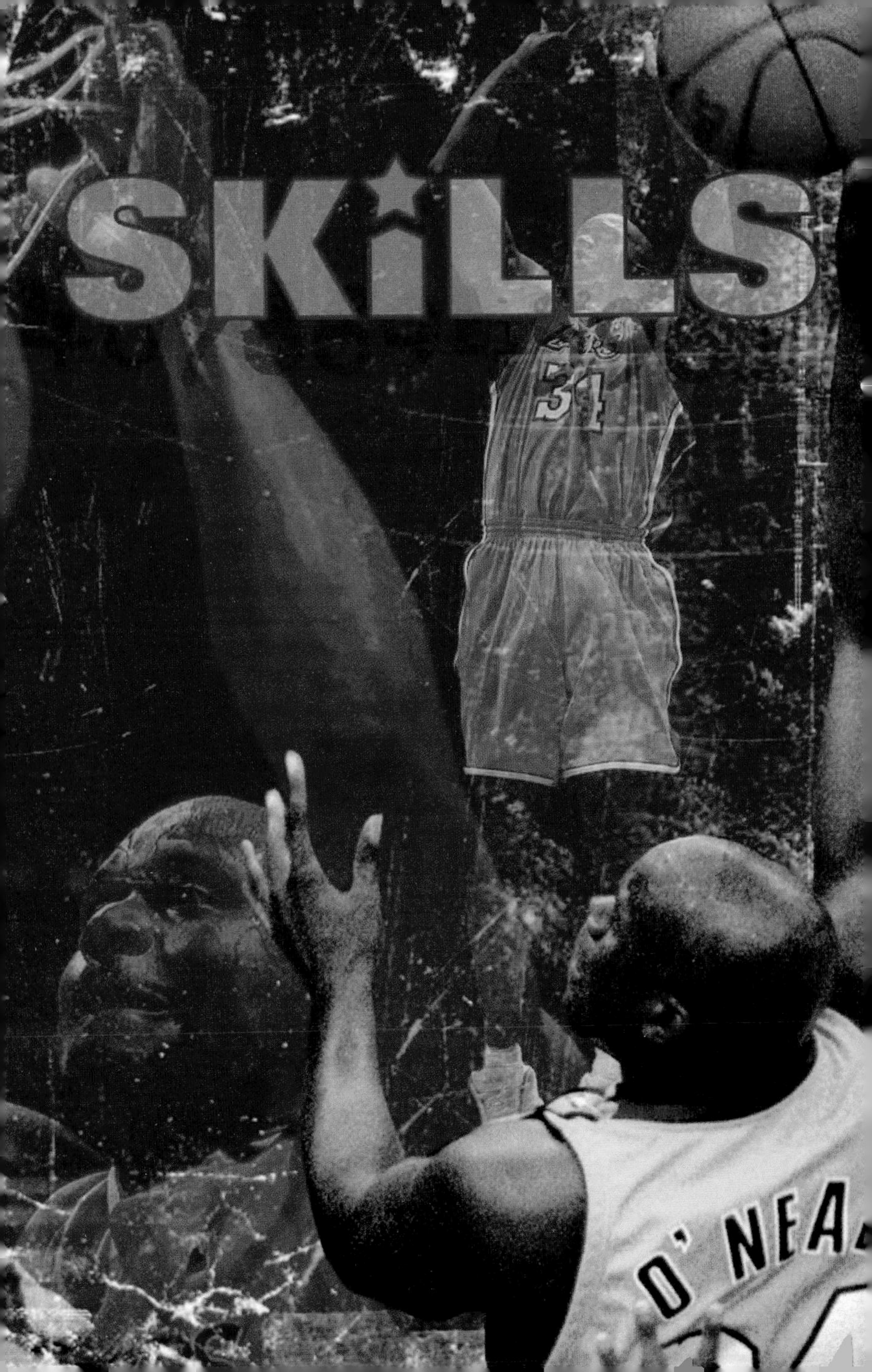
34
O' NEA

skills

POWER IN THE PAINT

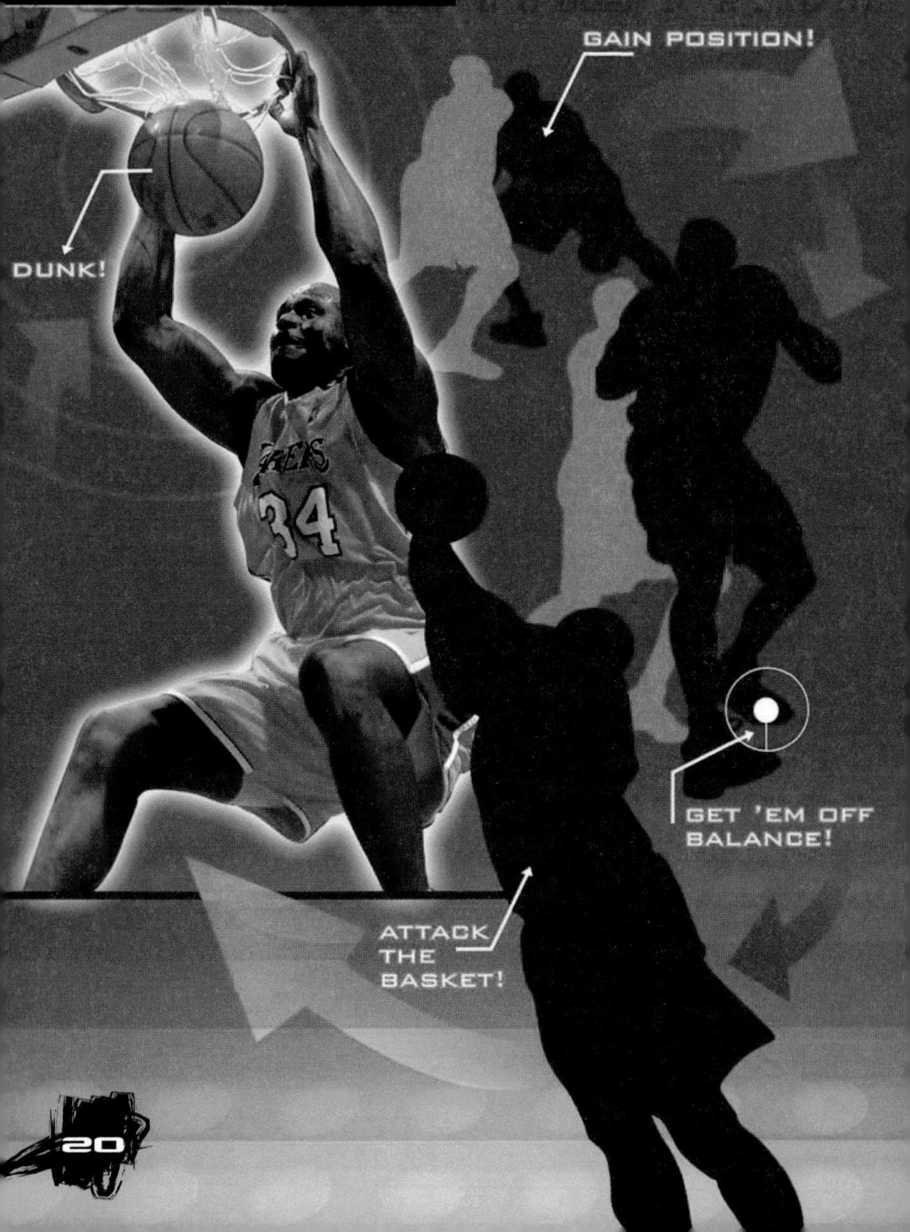
GAIN POSITION!
DUNK!
GET 'EM OFF BALANCE!
ATTACK THE BASKET!

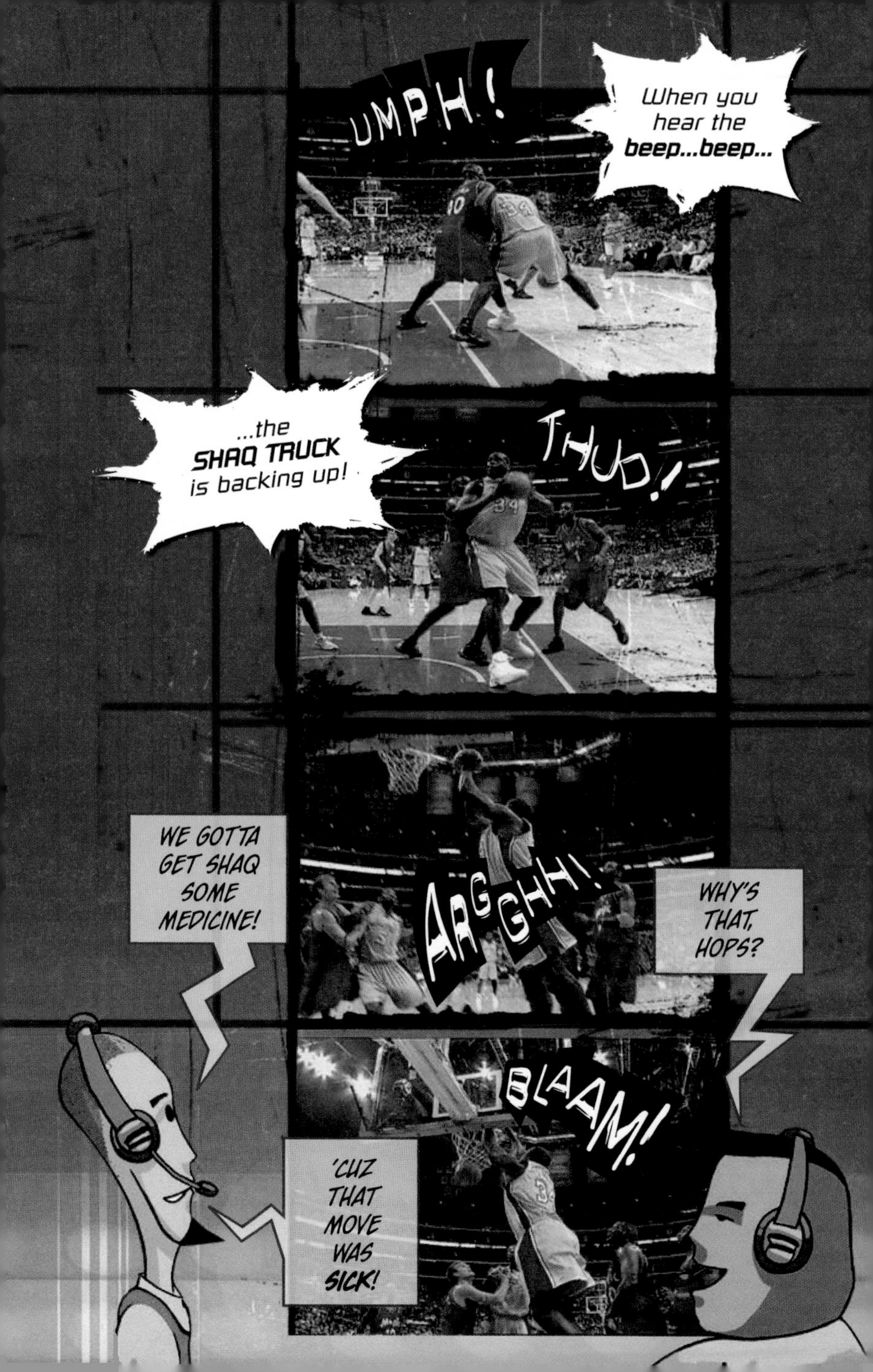
UMPH!
When you hear the beep...beep...
...the SHAQ TRUCK is backing up!
THUD!
WE GOTTA GET SHAQ SOME MEDICINE!
ARGGHH!
WHY'S THAT, HOPS?
BLAAM!
'CUZ THAT MOVE WAS SICK!

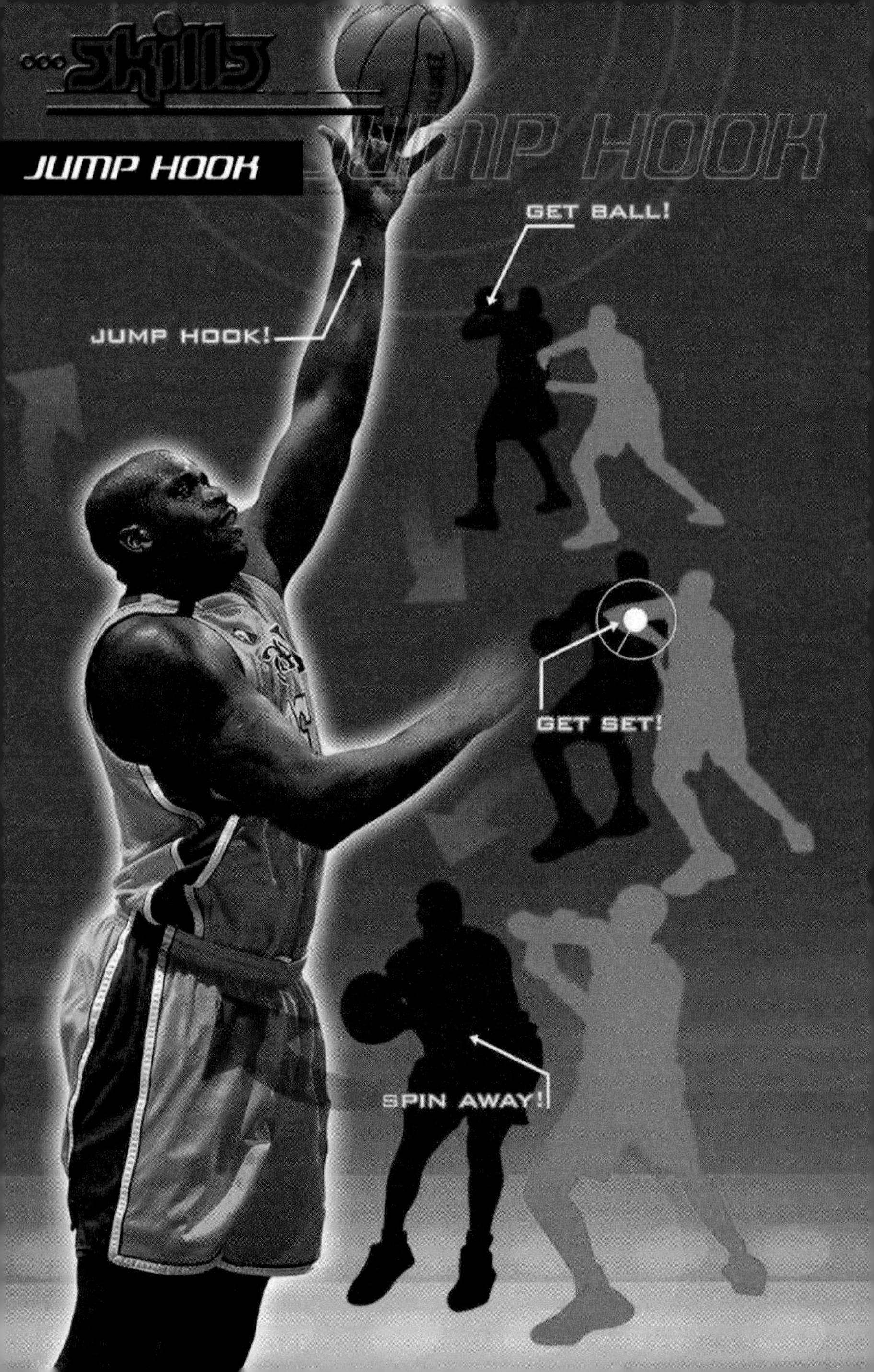
SKILLS
JUMP HOOK
JUMP HOOK
GET BALL!
JUMP HOOK!
GET SET!
SPIN AWAY!

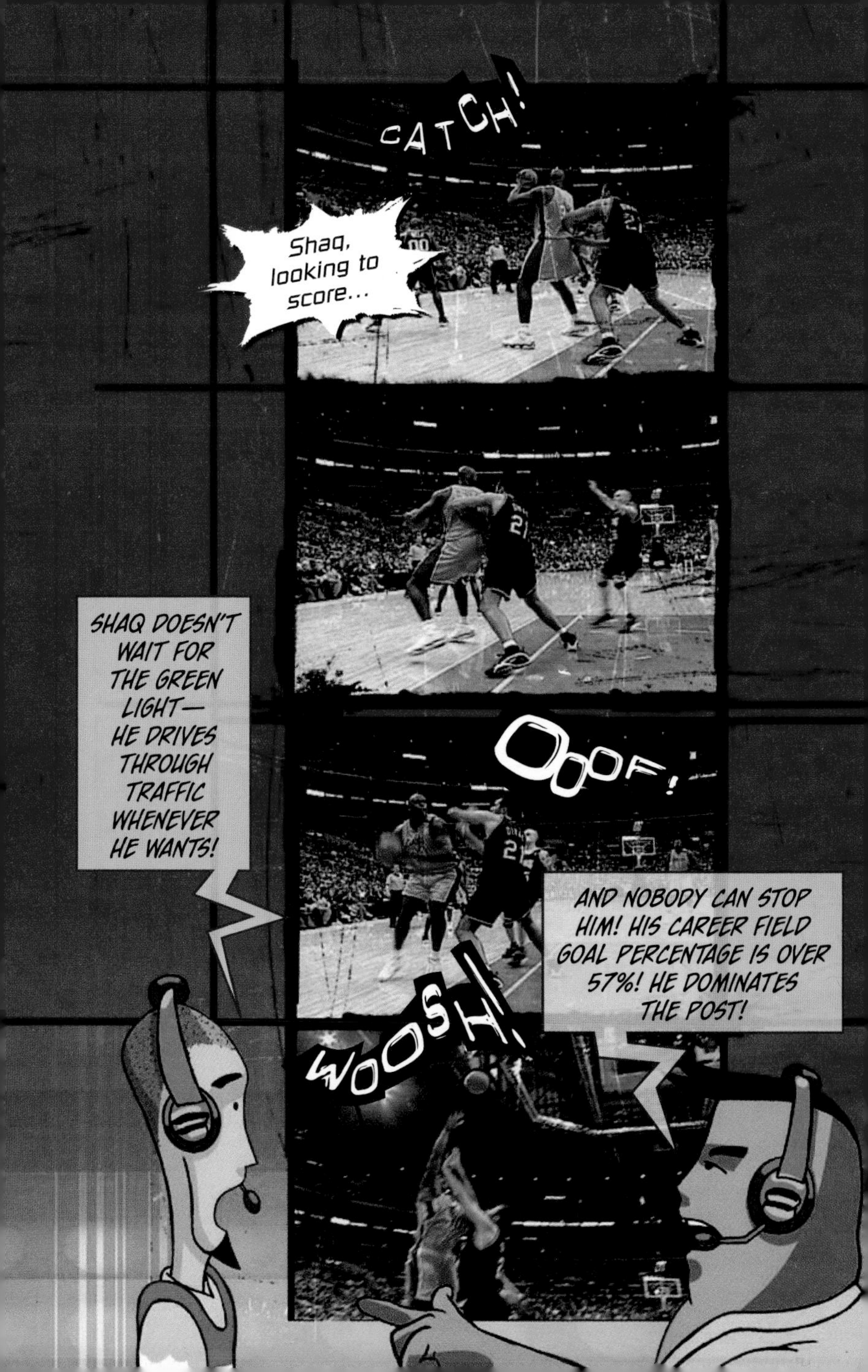
CATCH!
Shaq, looking to score...
SHAQ DOESN'T WAIT FOR THE GREEN LIGHT— HE DRIVES THROUGH TRAFFIC WHENEVER HE WANTS!
OOOOF!
AND NOBODY CAN STOP HIM! HIS CAREER FIELD GOAL PERCENTAGE IS OVER 57%! HE DOMINATES THE POST!
WOOSH!

MOST IN THE POST

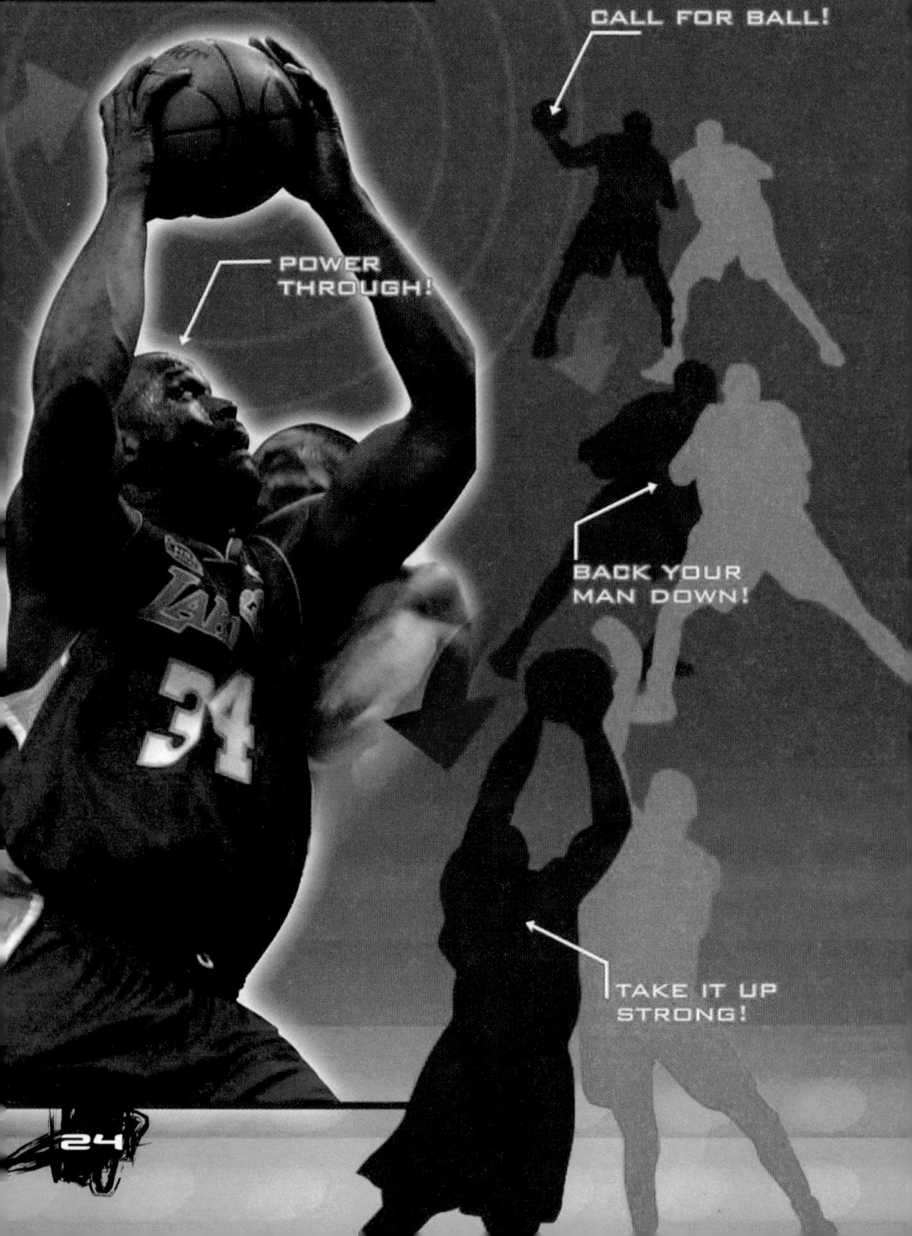
CALL FOR BALL!
POWER THROUGH!
BACK YOUR MAN DOWN!
TAKE IT UP STRONG!

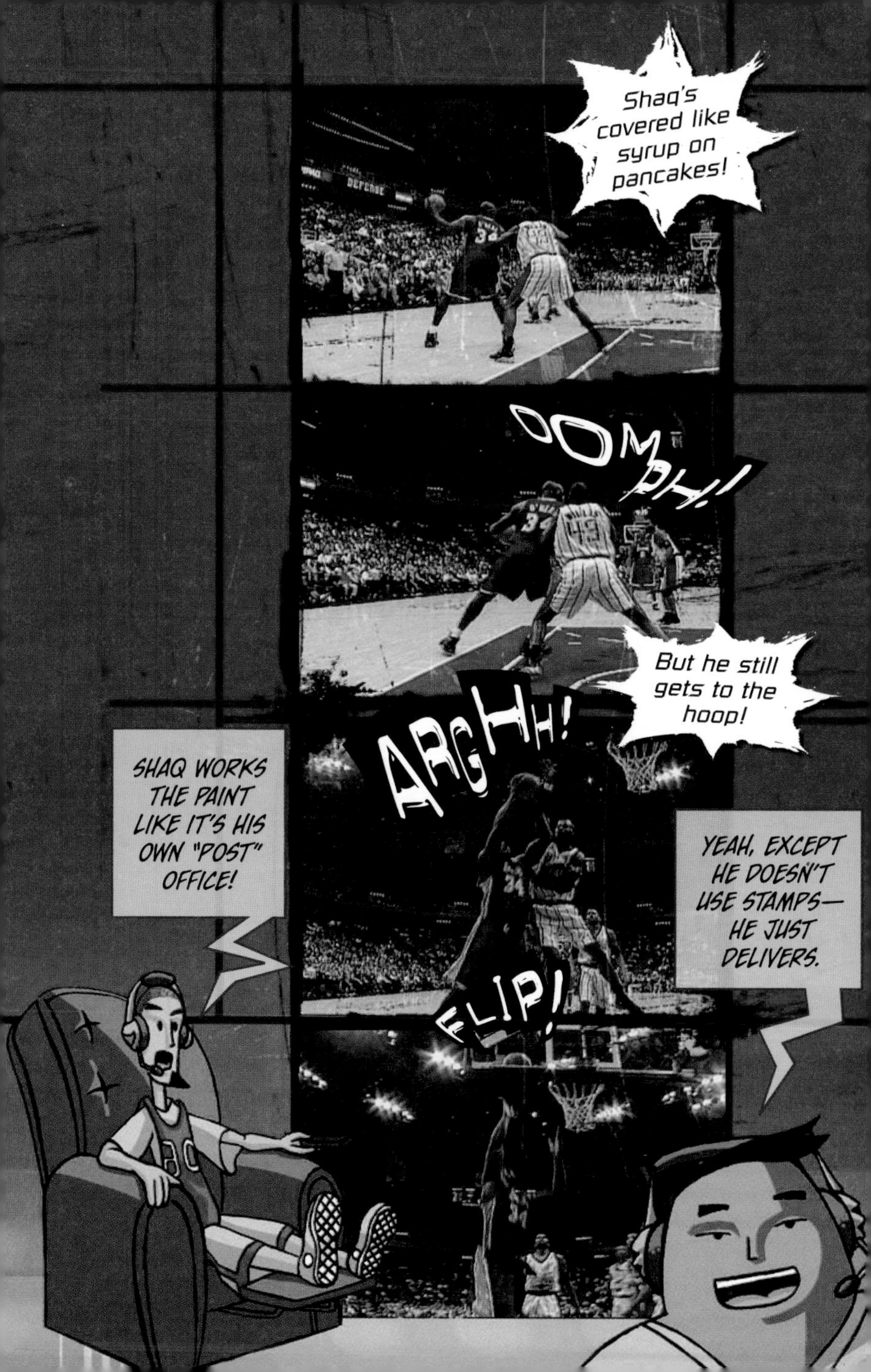
Shaq's covered like syrup on pancakes!
OOMPH!
But he still gets to the hoop!
ARGHH!
SHAQ WORKS THE PAINT LIKE IT'S HIS OWN "POST" OFFICE!
YEAH, EXCEPT HE DOESN'T USE STAMPS— HE JUST DELIVERS.
FLIP!

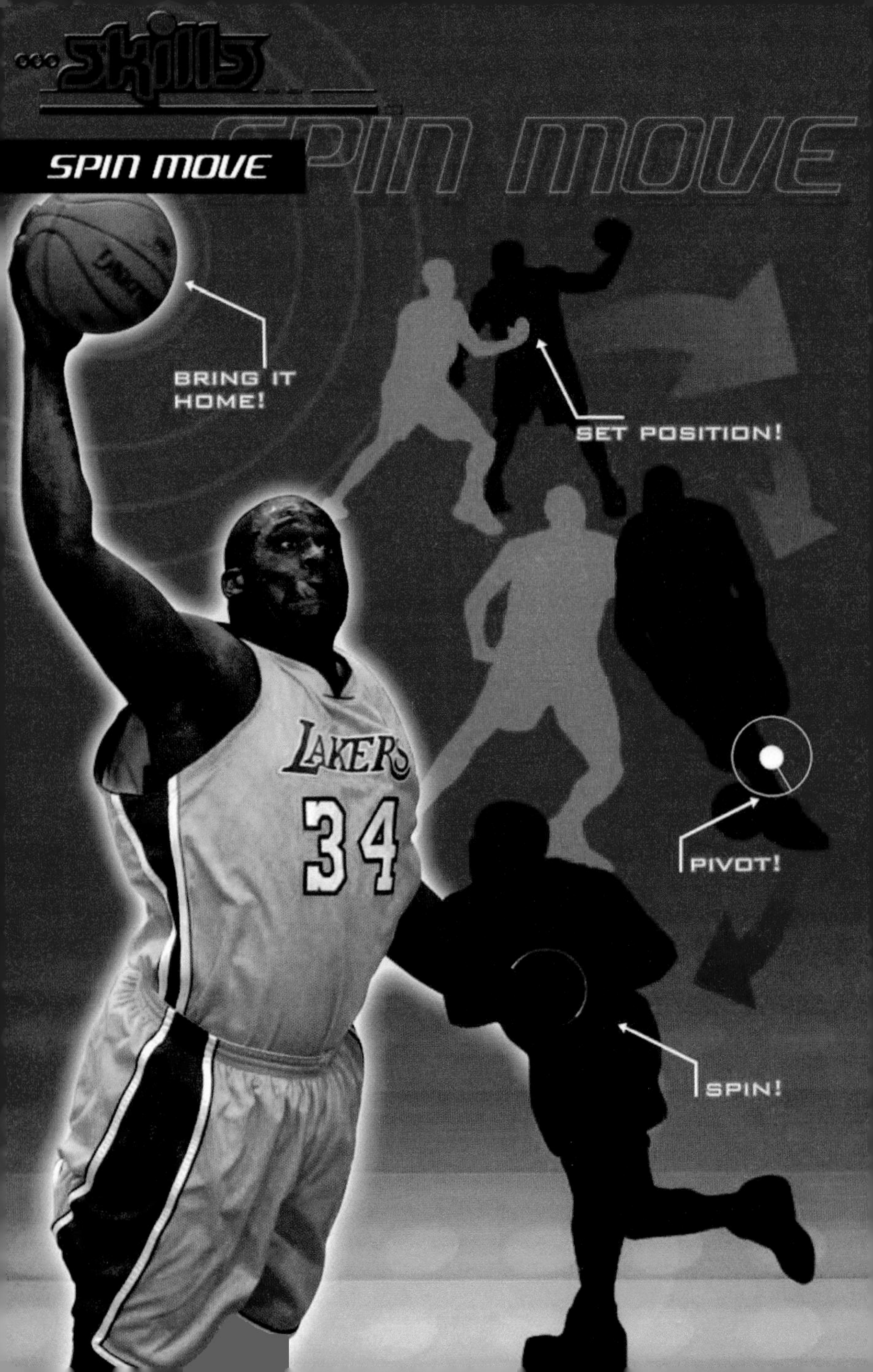
...skills
SPIN MOVE
SPIN MOVE
BRING IT
HOME!
SET POSITION!
LAKERS
34
PIVOT!
SPIN!

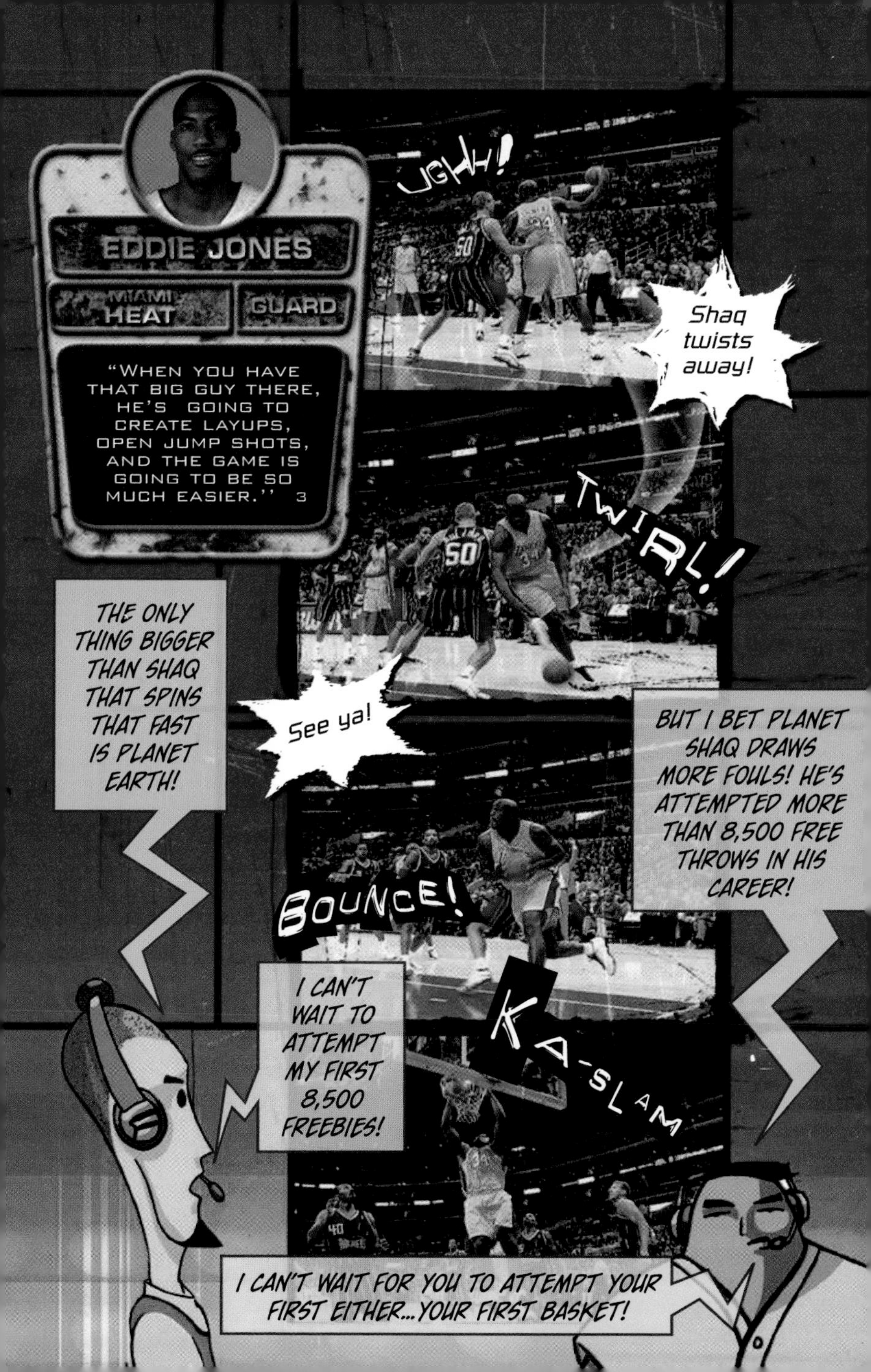
EDDIE JONES
MIAMI HEAT
GUARD
"WHEN YOU HAVE THAT BIG GUY THERE, HE'S GOING TO CREATE LAYUPS, OPEN JUMP SHOTS, AND THE GAME IS GOING TO BE SO MUCH EASIER." 3
UGHH!
Shaq twists away!
TWIRL!
THE ONLY THING BIGGER THAN SHAQ THAT SPINS THAT FAST IS PLANET EARTH!
See ya!
BUT I BET PLANET SHAQ DRAWS MORE FOULS! HE'S ATTEMPTED MORE THAN 8,500 FREE THROWS IN HIS CAREER!
BOUNCE!
I CAN'T WAIT TO ATTEMPT MY FIRST 8,500 FREEBIES!
KA-SLAM
I CAN'T WAIT FOR YOU TO ATTEMPT YOUR FIRST EITHER...YOUR FIRST BASKET!

ALLEY OOP

ALLEY OOP

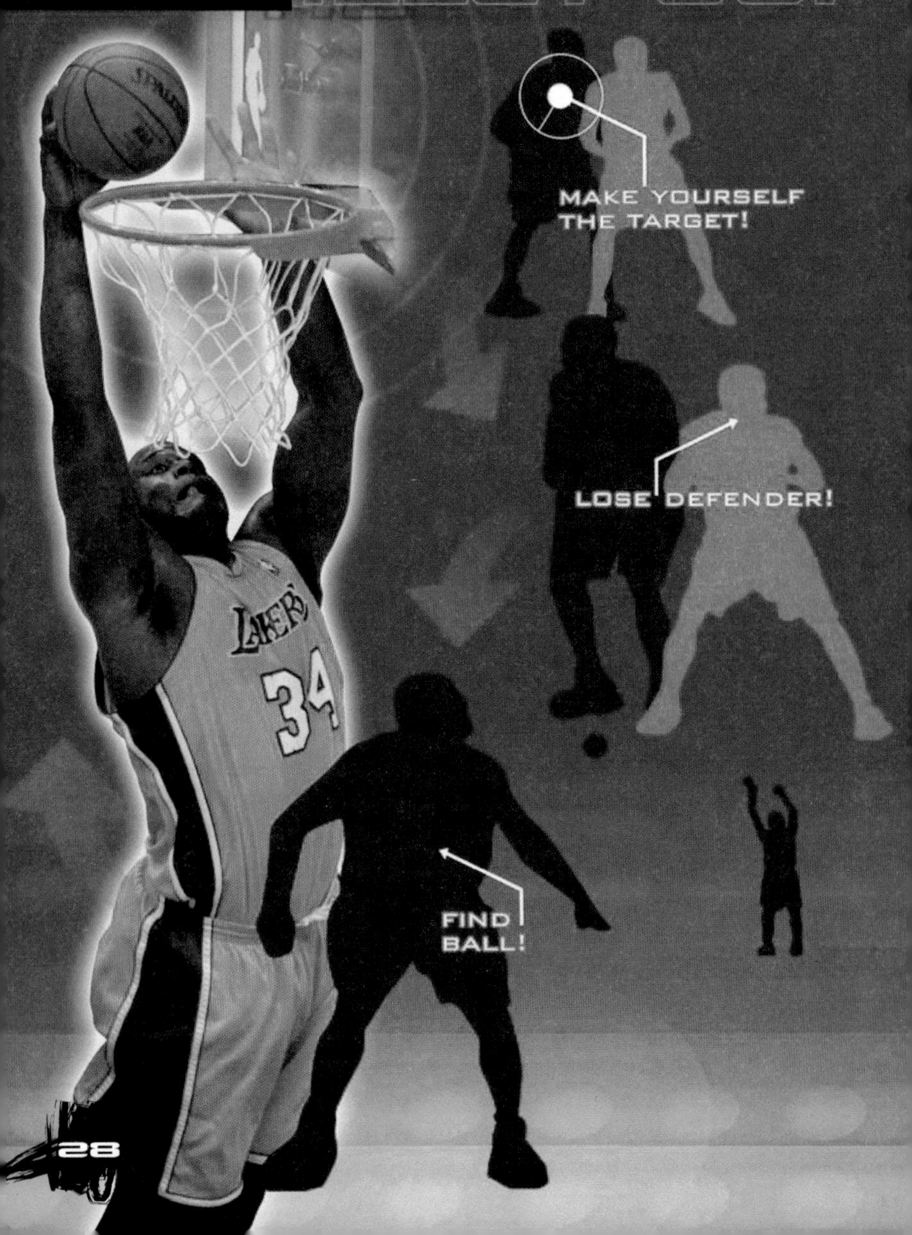
MAKE YOURSELF THE TARGET!
LOSE DEFENDER!
FIND BALL!

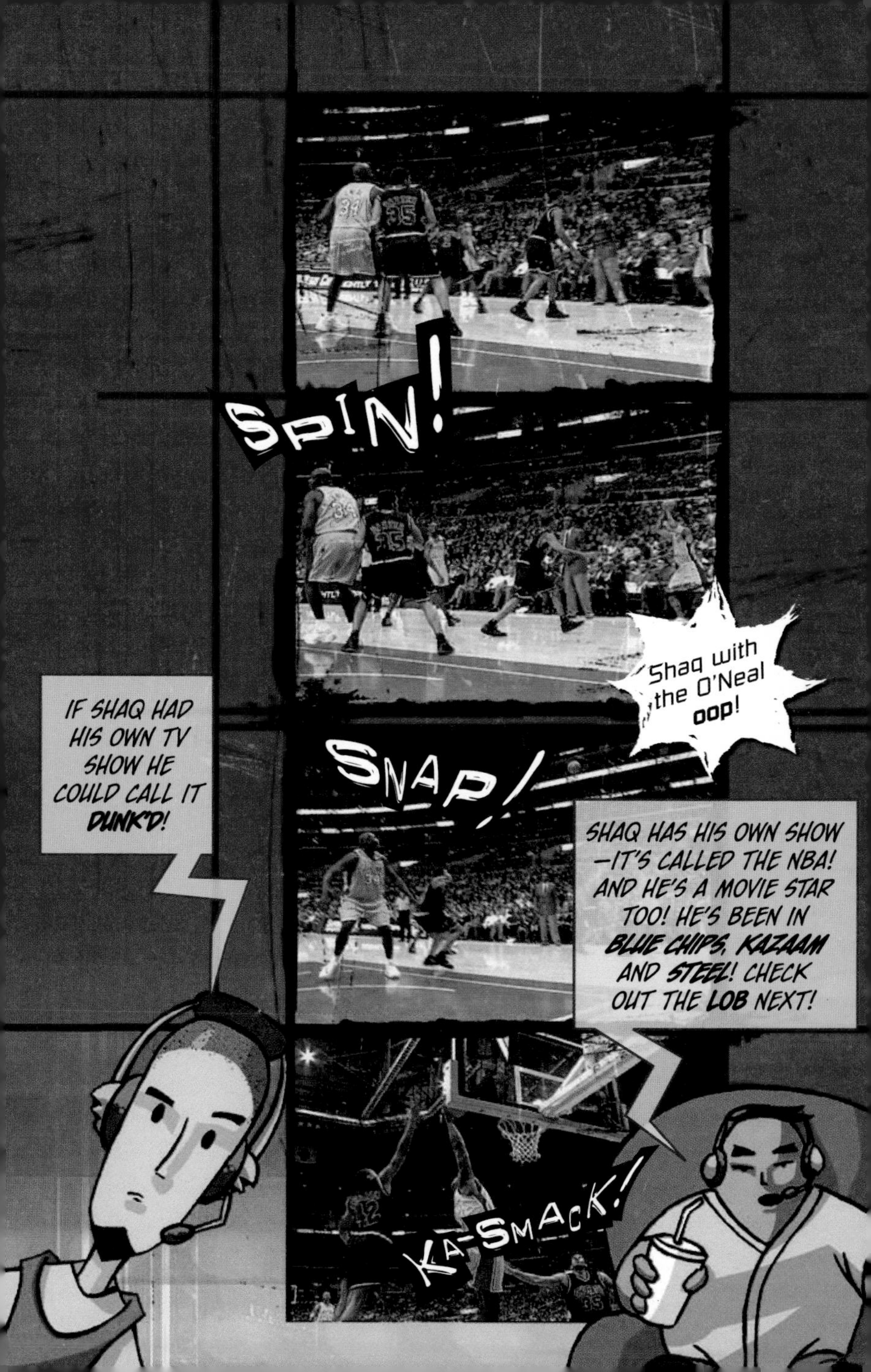
SPIN!
Shaq with the O'Neal oop!
IF SHAQ HAD HIS OWN TV SHOW HE COULD CALL IT DUNK'D!
SNAP!
SHAQ HAS HIS OWN SHOW —IT'S CALLED THE NBA! AND HE'S A MOVIE STAR TOO! HE'S BEEN IN BLUE CHIPS, KAZAAM AND STEEL! CHECK OUT THE LOB NEXT!
KA-SMACK!

THE LOB

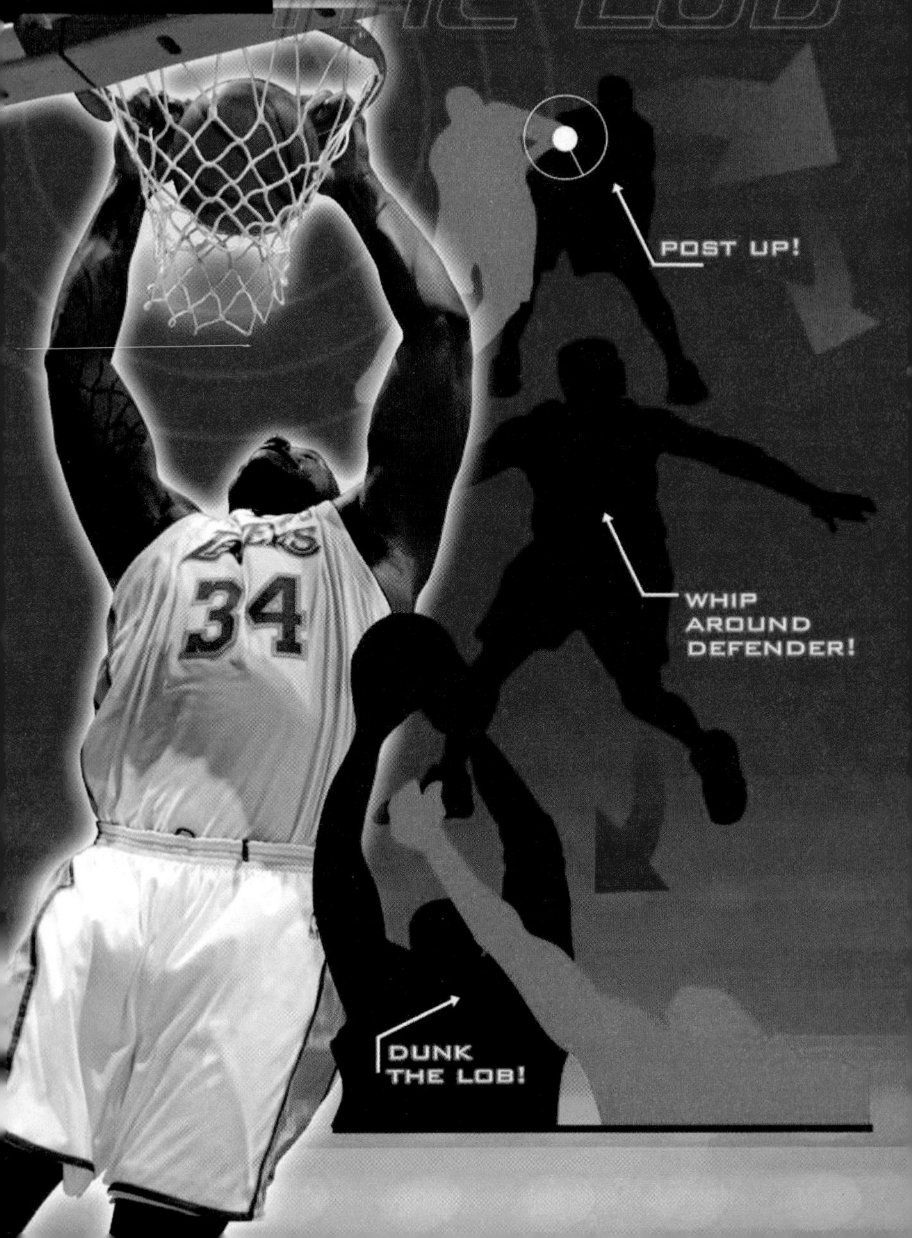
THE LOB
34
POST UP!
WHIP
AROUND
DEFENDER!
DUNK
THE LOB!

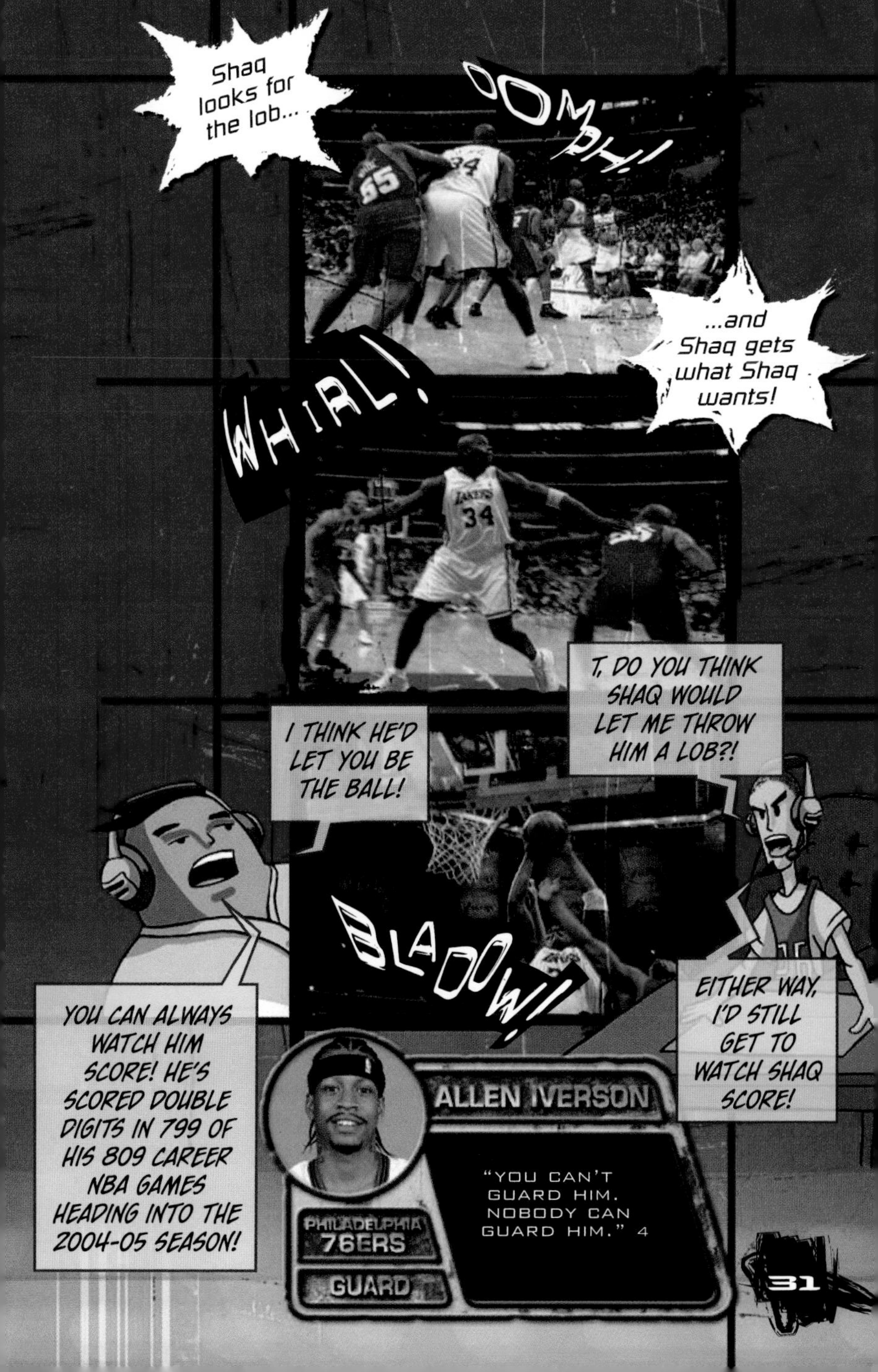

Shaq looks for the lob...
OOMPH!
WHIRL!
...and Shaq gets what Shaq wants!
I THINK HE'D LET YOU BE THE BALL!
T, DO YOU THINK SHAQ WOULD LET ME THROW HIM A LOB?!
BLADOOW!
YOU CAN ALWAYS WATCH HIM SCORE! HE'S SCORED DOUBLE DIGITS IN 799 OF HIS 809 CAREER NBA GAMES HEADING INTO THE 2004-05 SEASON!
EITHER WAY, I'D STILL GET TO WATCH SHAQ SCORE!
ALLEN IVERSON
PHILADELPHIA 76ERS
GUARD
"YOU CAN'T GUARD HIM. NOBODY CAN GUARD HIM." 4

skills

TURNAROUND JUMPER

TURNAROUND J

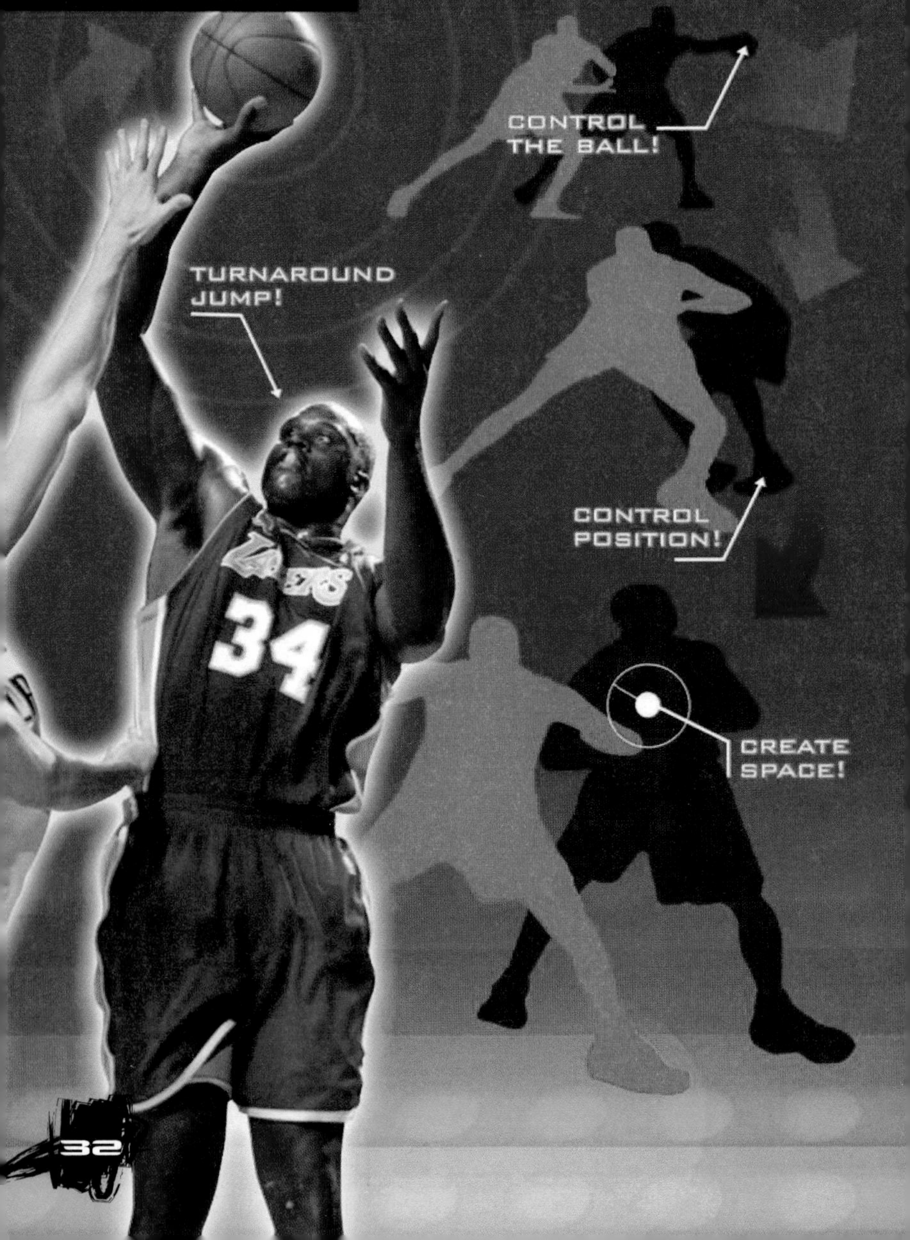
CONTROL
THE BALL!
TURNAROUND
JUMP!
CONTROL
POSITION!
CREATE
SPACE!

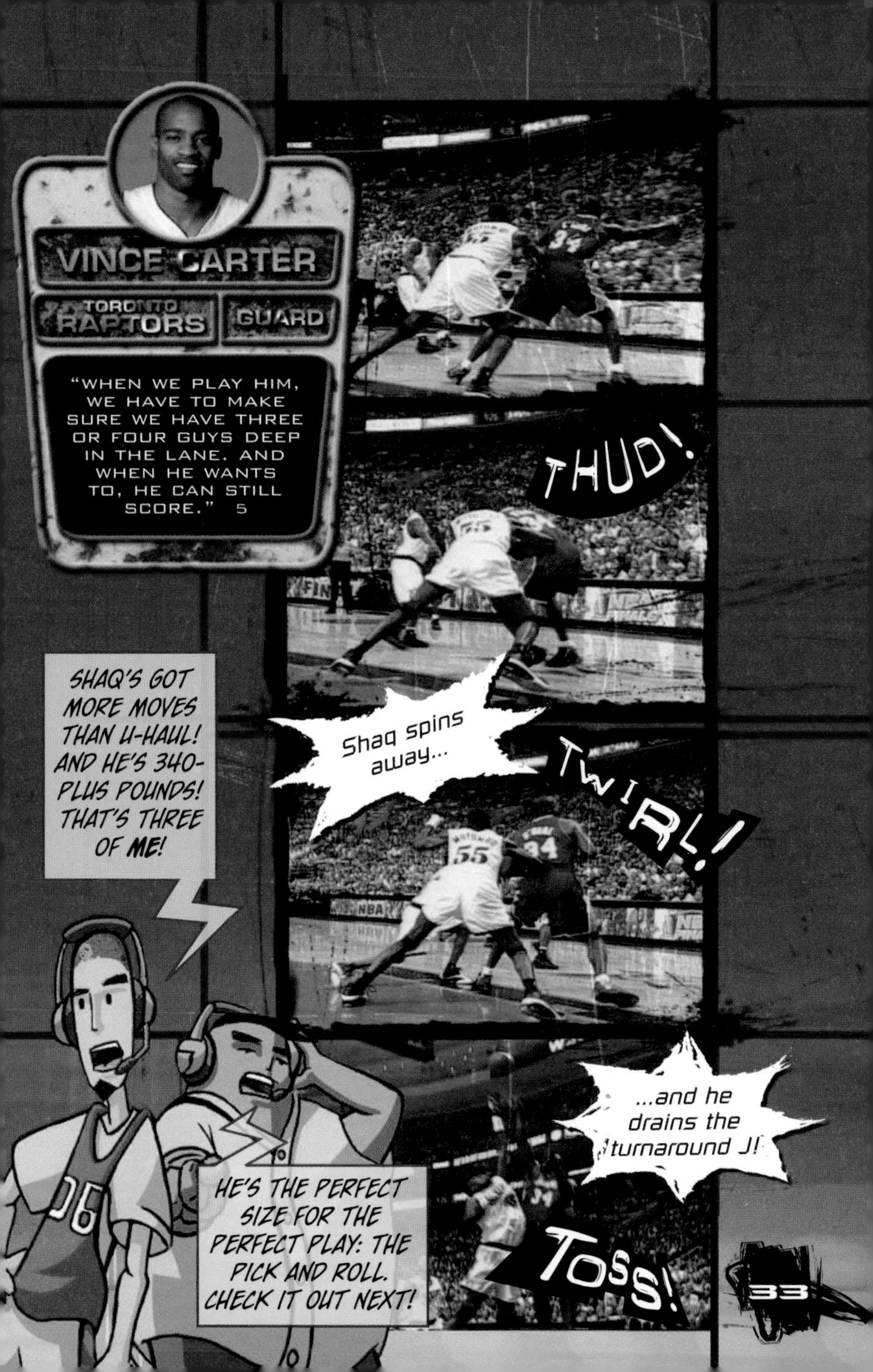
VINCE CARTER
TORONTO RAPTORS
GUARD
"WHEN WE PLAY HIM, WE HAVE TO MAKE SURE WE HAVE THREE OR FOUR GUYS DEEP IN THE LANE. AND WHEN HE WANTS TO, HE CAN STILL SCORE." 5
THUD!
SHAQ'S GOT MORE MOVES THAN U-HAUL! AND HE'S 340-PLUS POUNDS! THAT'S THREE OF **ME!**
Shaq spins away...
TWIRL!
...and he drains the turnaround J!
HE'S THE PERFECT SIZE FOR THE PERFECT PLAY: THE PICK AND ROLL. CHECK IT OUT NEXT!
TOSS!

PICK AND ROLL

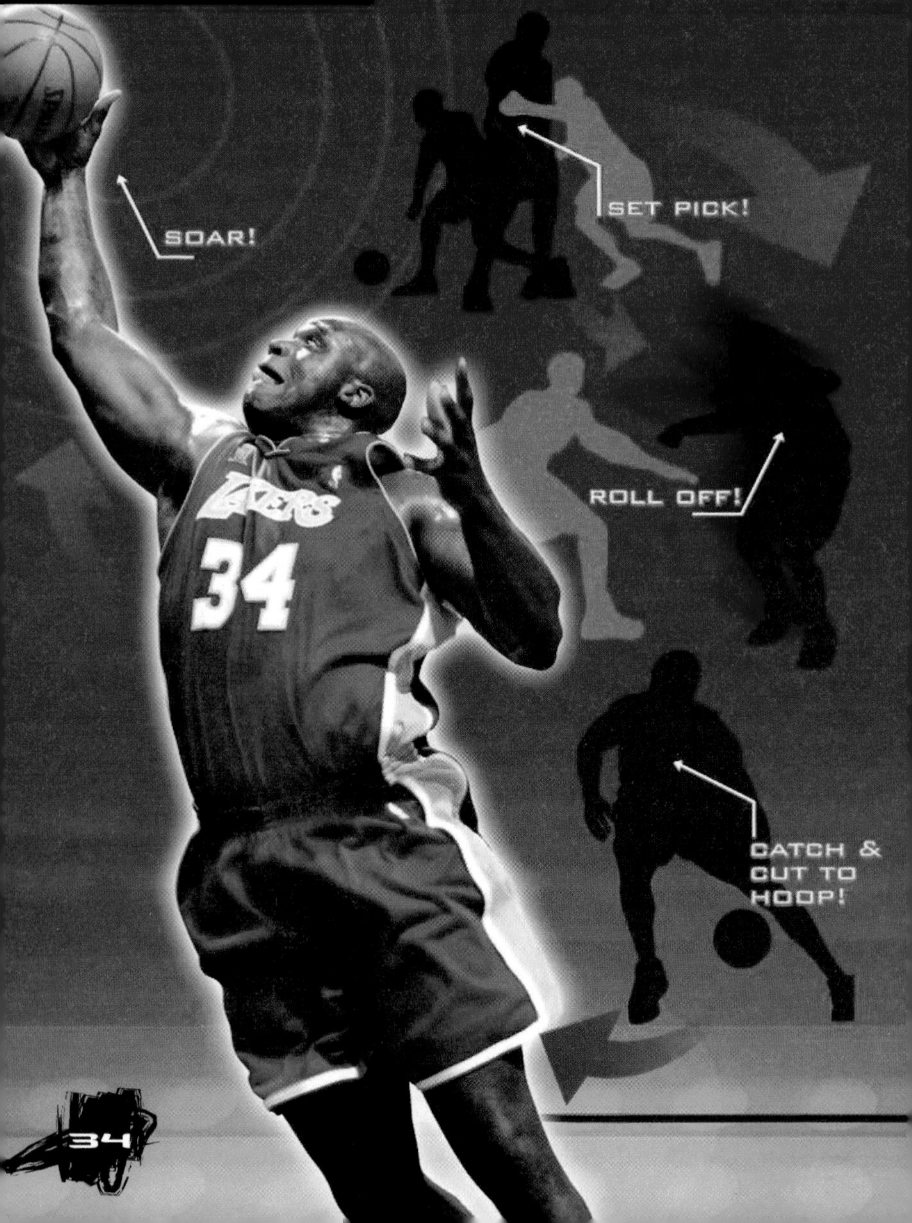
PICK AND ROLL
SET PICK!
SOAR!
ROLL OFF!
CATCH & CUT TO HOOP!
LAKERS
34

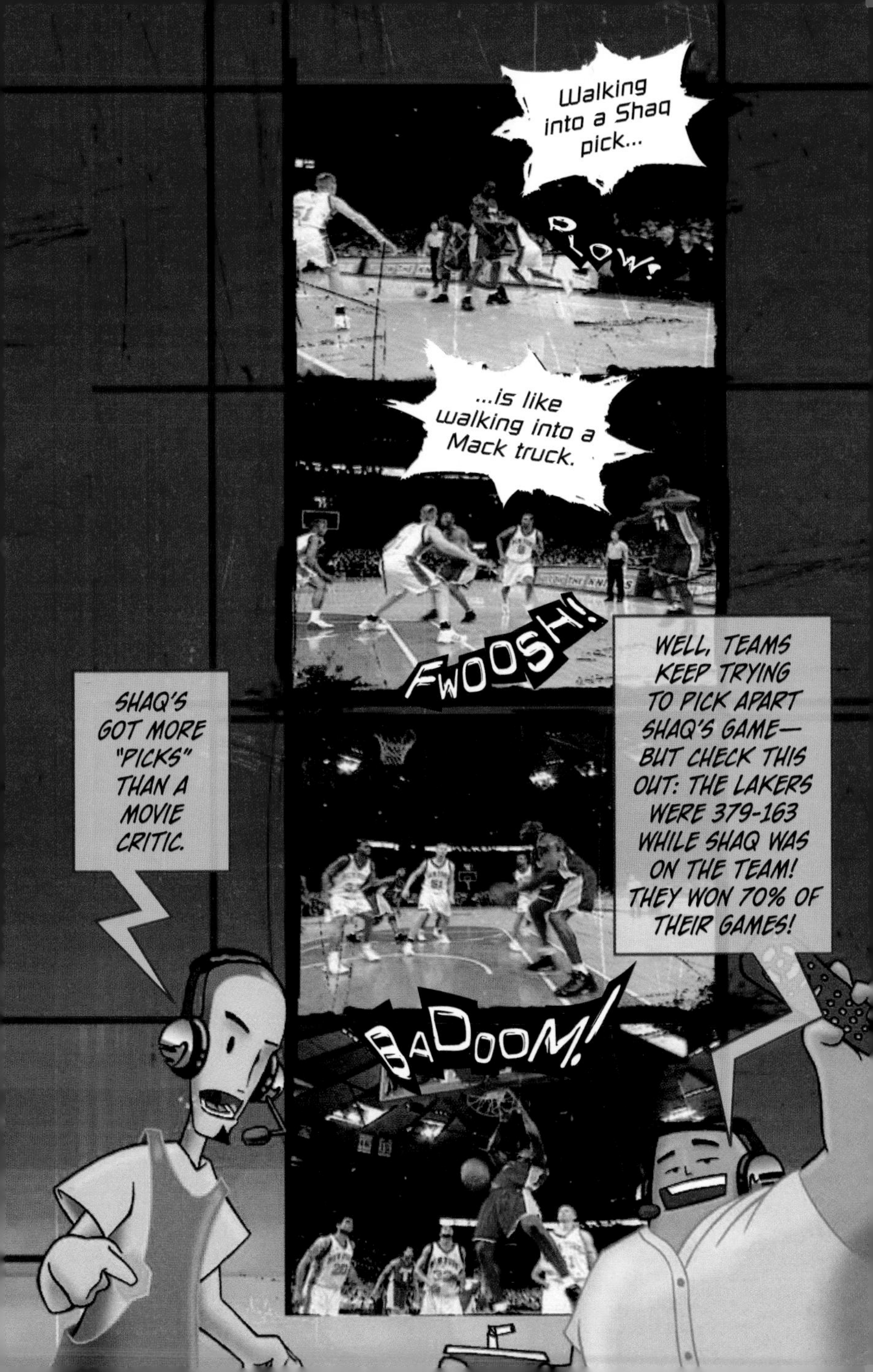
Walking into a Shaq pick...
PLOW!
...is like walking into a Mack truck.
FWOOSH!
SHAQ'S GOT MORE "PICKS" THAN A MOVIE CRITIC.
WELL, TEAMS KEEP TRYING TO PICK APART SHAQ'S GAME—BUT CHECK THIS OUT: THE LAKERS WERE 379-163 WHILE SHAQ WAS ON THE TEAM! THEY WON 70% OF THEIR GAMES!
BADOOM!

BLOCKS

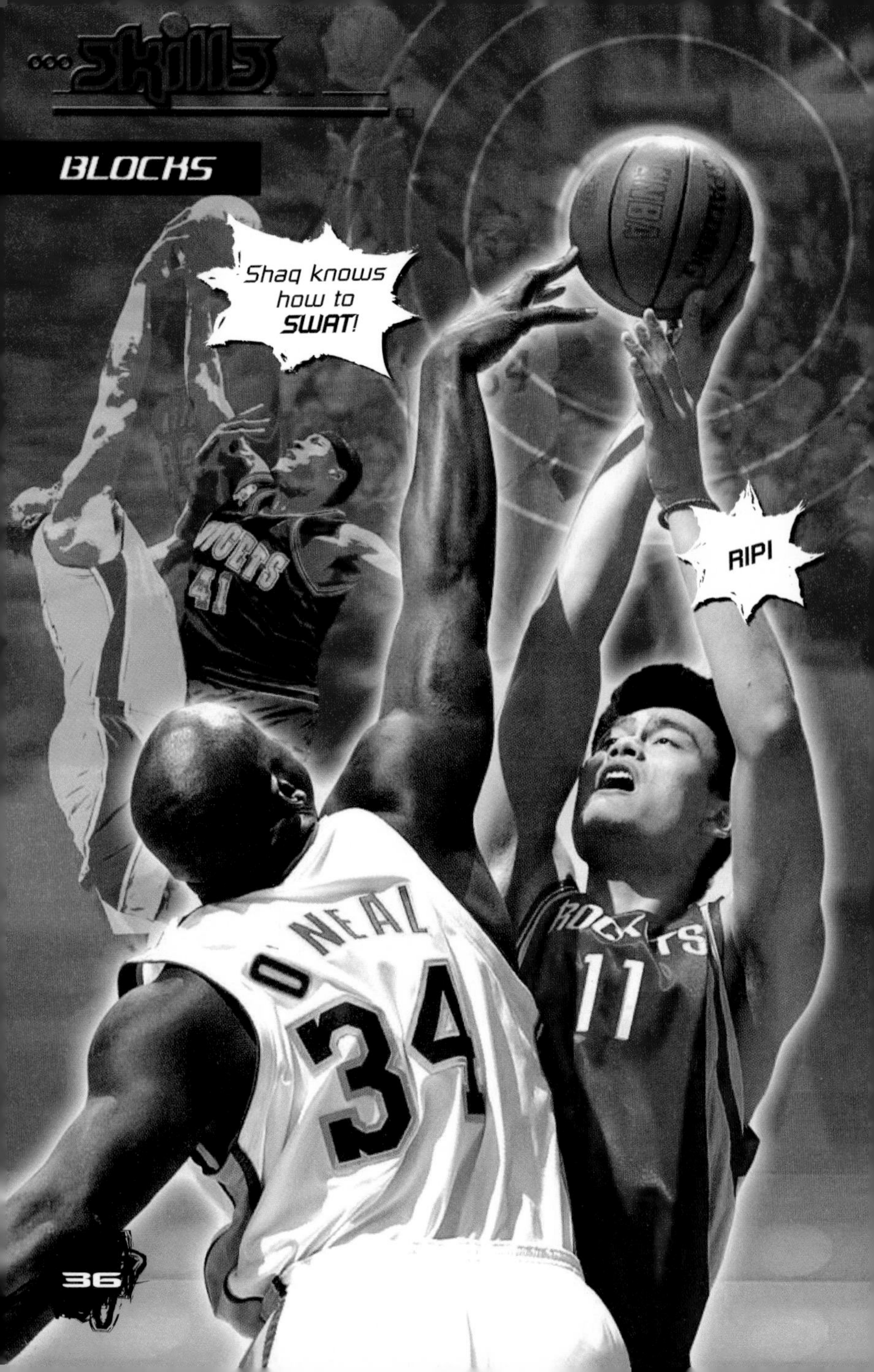
Shaq knows how to **SWAT**!
RIP!
O'NEAL 34
ROCKETS 11
41

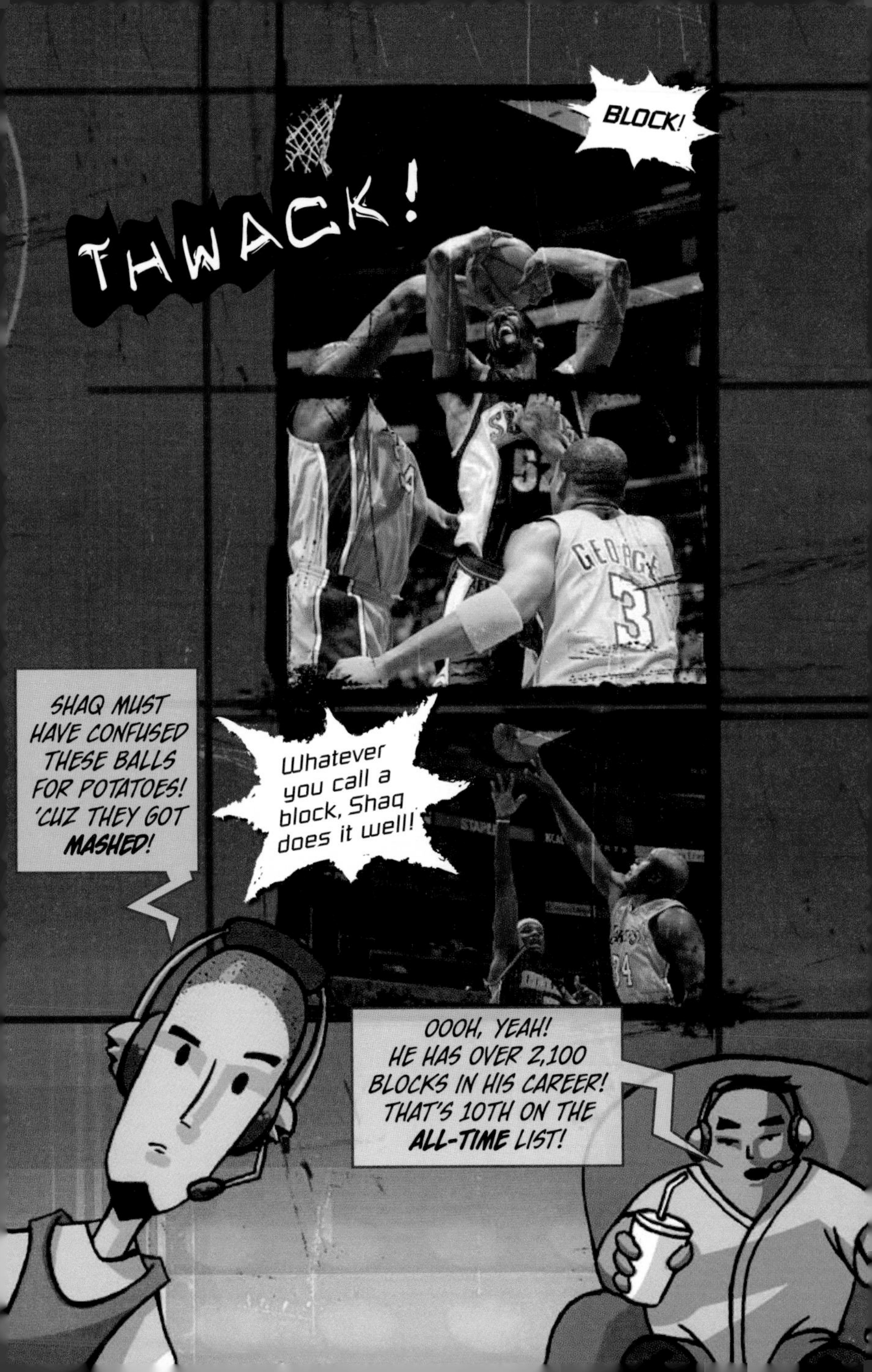
BLOCK!
THWACK!
SHAQ MUST HAVE CONFUSED THESE BALLS FOR POTATOES! 'CUZ THEY GOT **MASHED**!
Whatever you call a block, Shaq does it well!
OOOH, YEAH! HE HAS OVER 2,100 BLOCKS IN HIS CAREER! THAT'S 10TH ON THE **ALL-TIME** LIST!

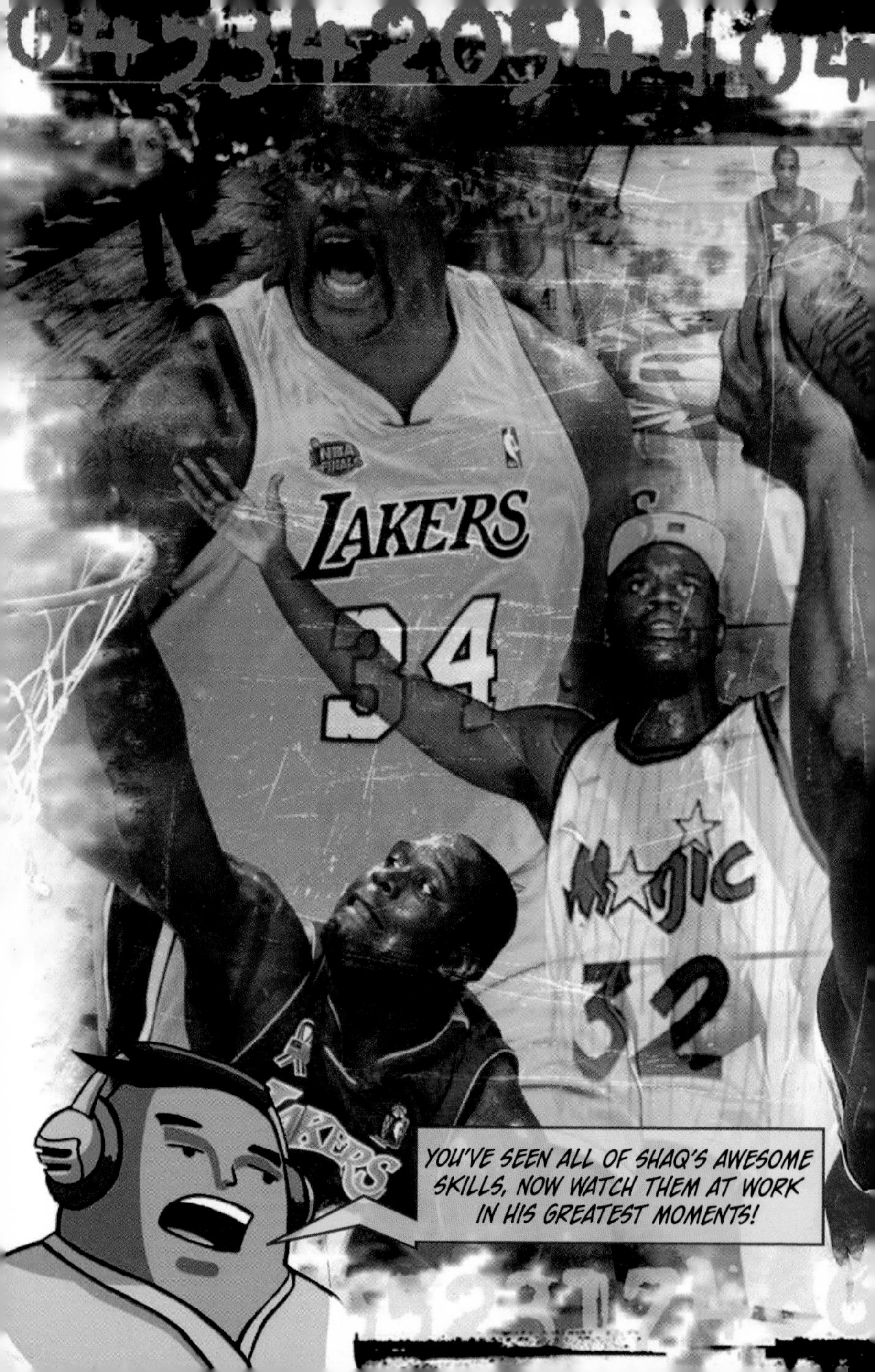
YOU'VE SEEN ALL OF SHAQ'S AWESOME SKILLS, NOW WATCH THEM AT WORK IN HIS GREATEST MOMENTS!

GREATEST MOMENTS

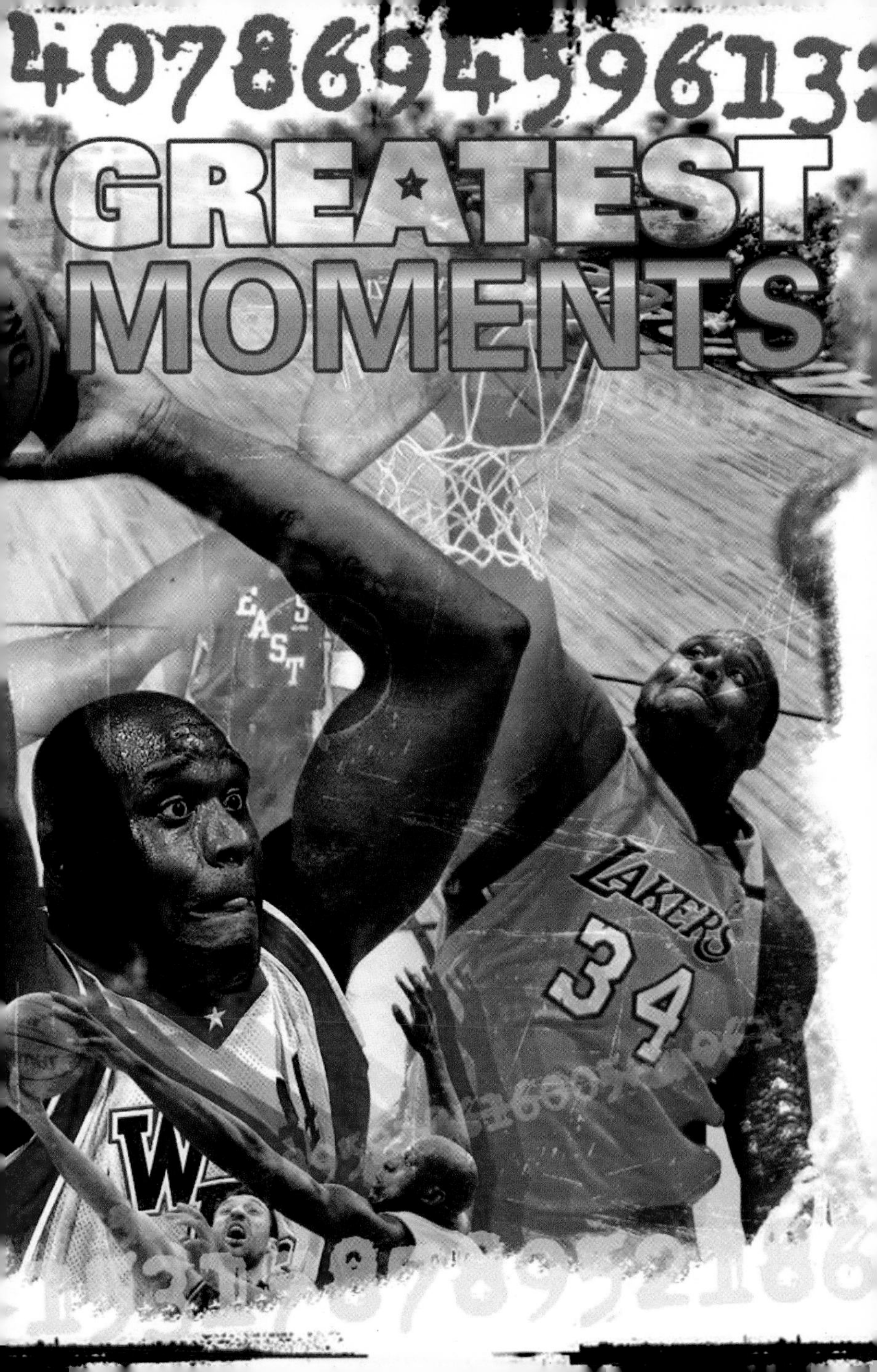

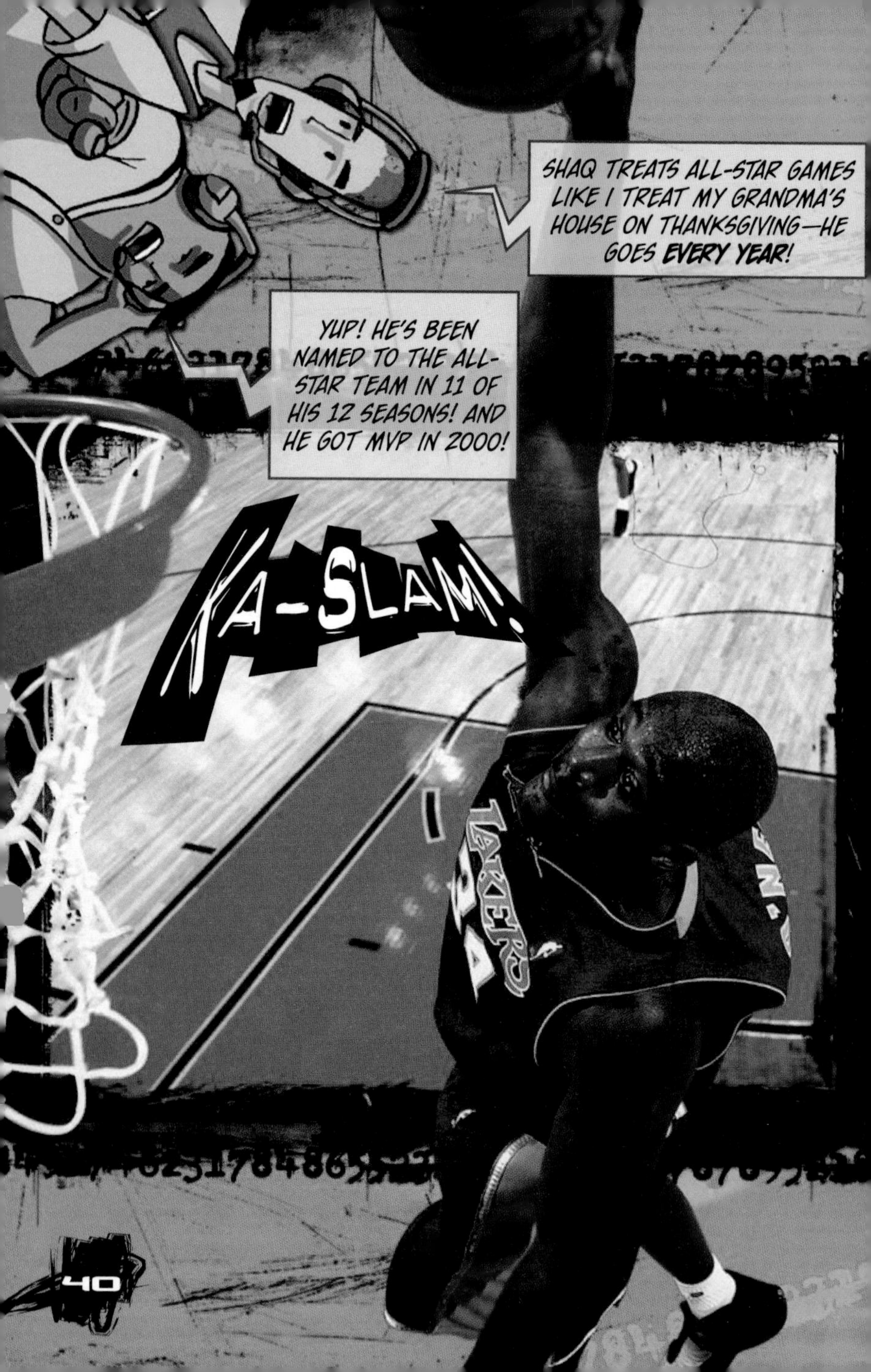
SHAQ TREATS ALL-STAR GAMES LIKE I TREAT MY GRANDMA'S HOUSE ON THANKSGIVING—HE GOES **EVERY YEAR!**
YUP! HE'S BEEN NAMED TO THE ALL-STAR TEAM IN 11 OF HIS 12 SEASONS! AND HE GOT MVP IN 2000!
KA-SLAM!
LAKERS

February 13, 2000:
NBA All-Star Game MVP!

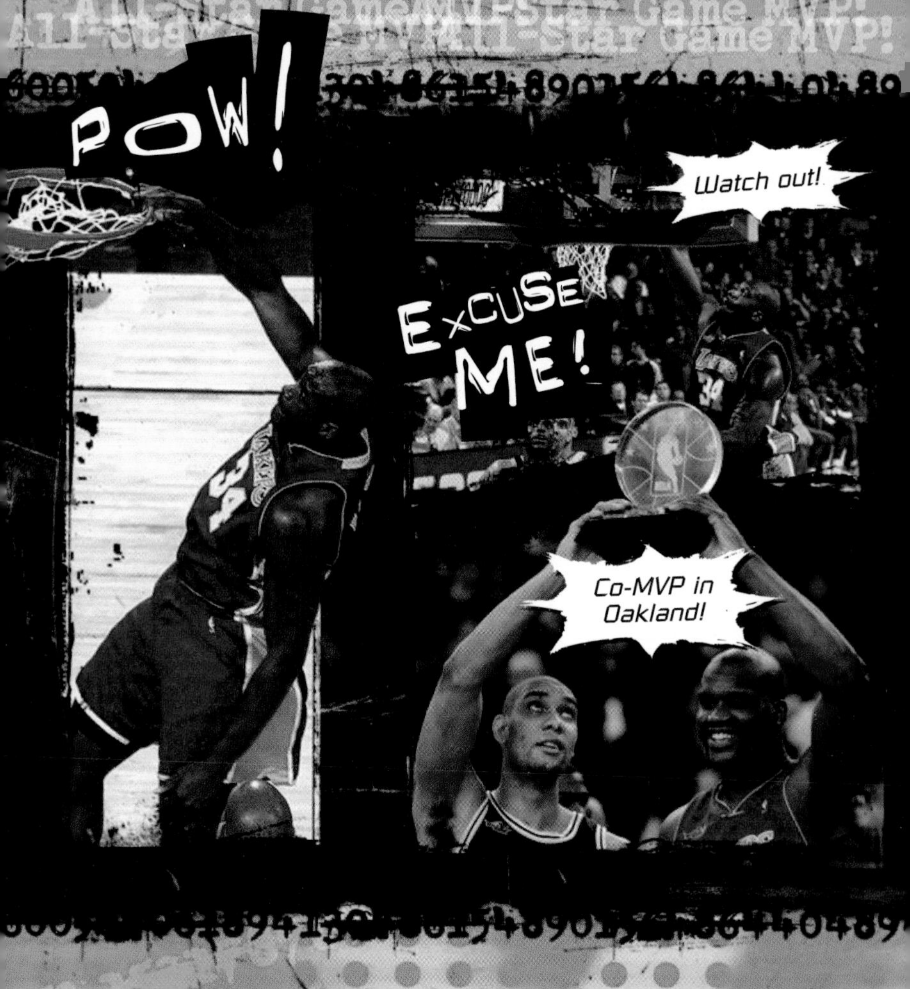
POW!
Watch out!
EXCUSE ME!
Co-MVP in Oakland!

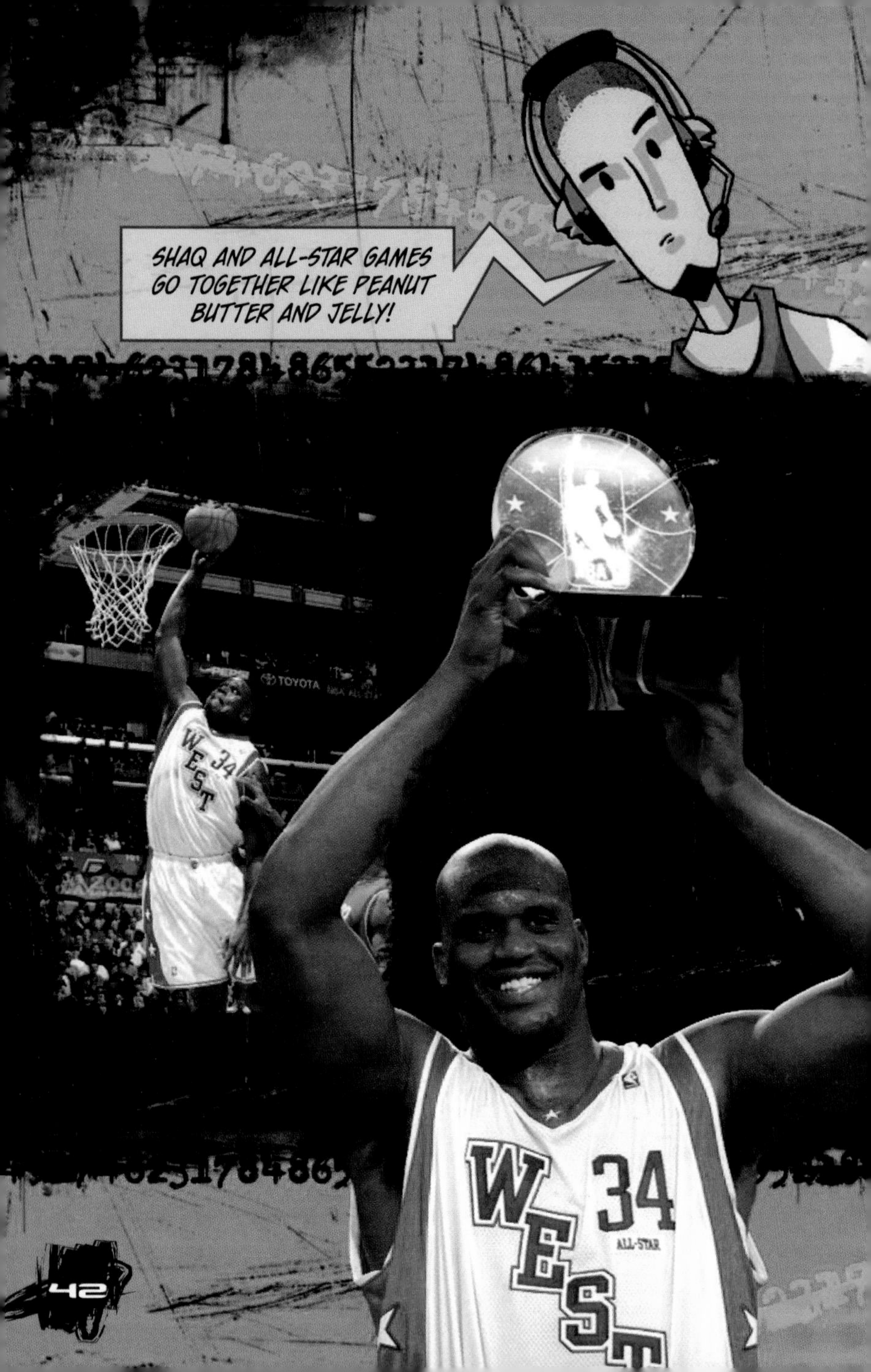
SHAQ AND ALL-STAR GAMES GO TOGETHER LIKE PEANUT BUTTER AND JELLY!

February 14, 2004:
NBA All-Star Game MVP!

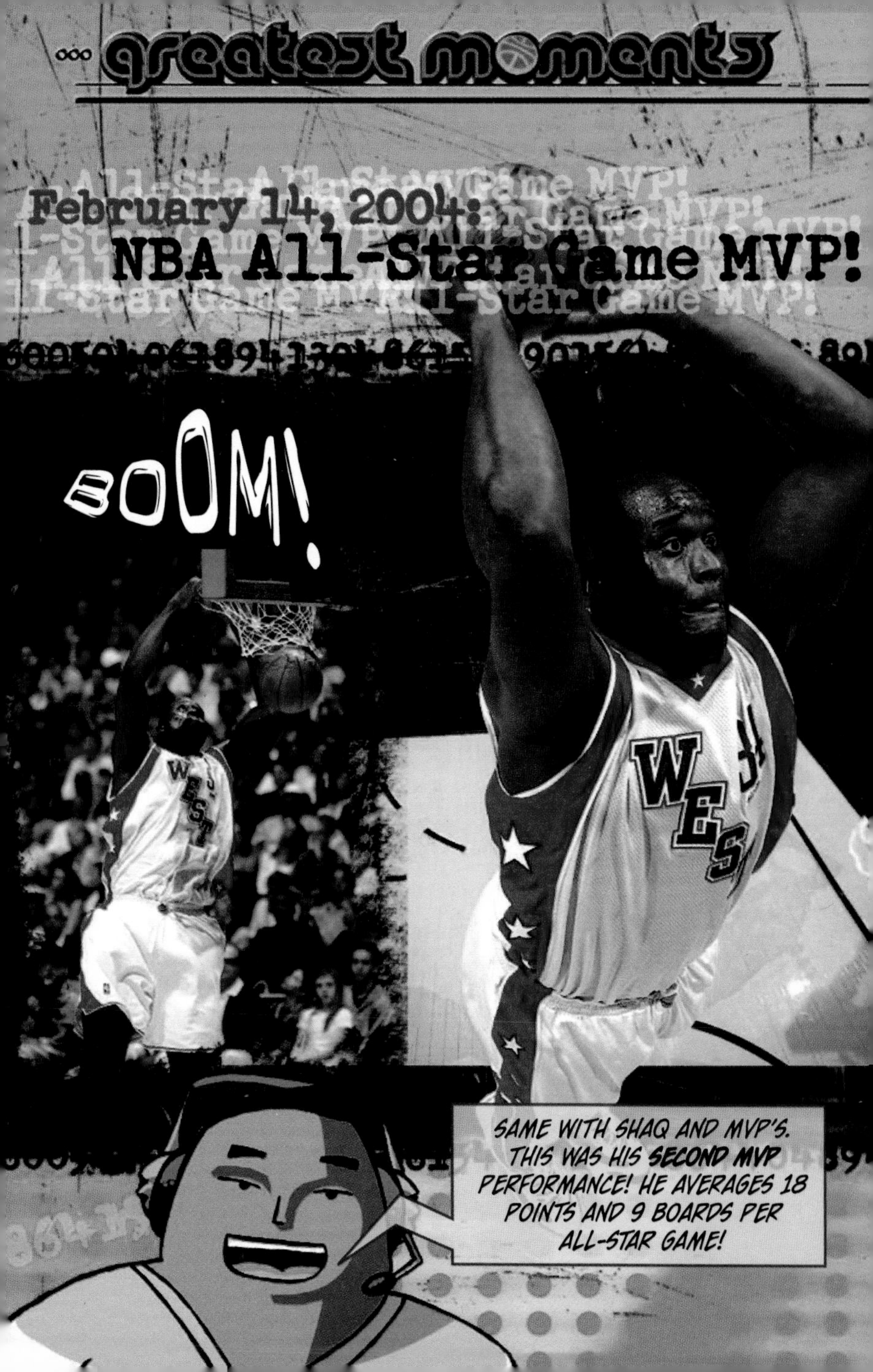
BOOM!
SAME WITH SHAQ AND MVP'S. THIS WAS HIS **SECOND MVP** PERFORMANCE! HE AVERAGES 18 POINTS AND 9 BOARDS PER ALL-STAR GAME!

November 6, 1992: Shaq's First Game!

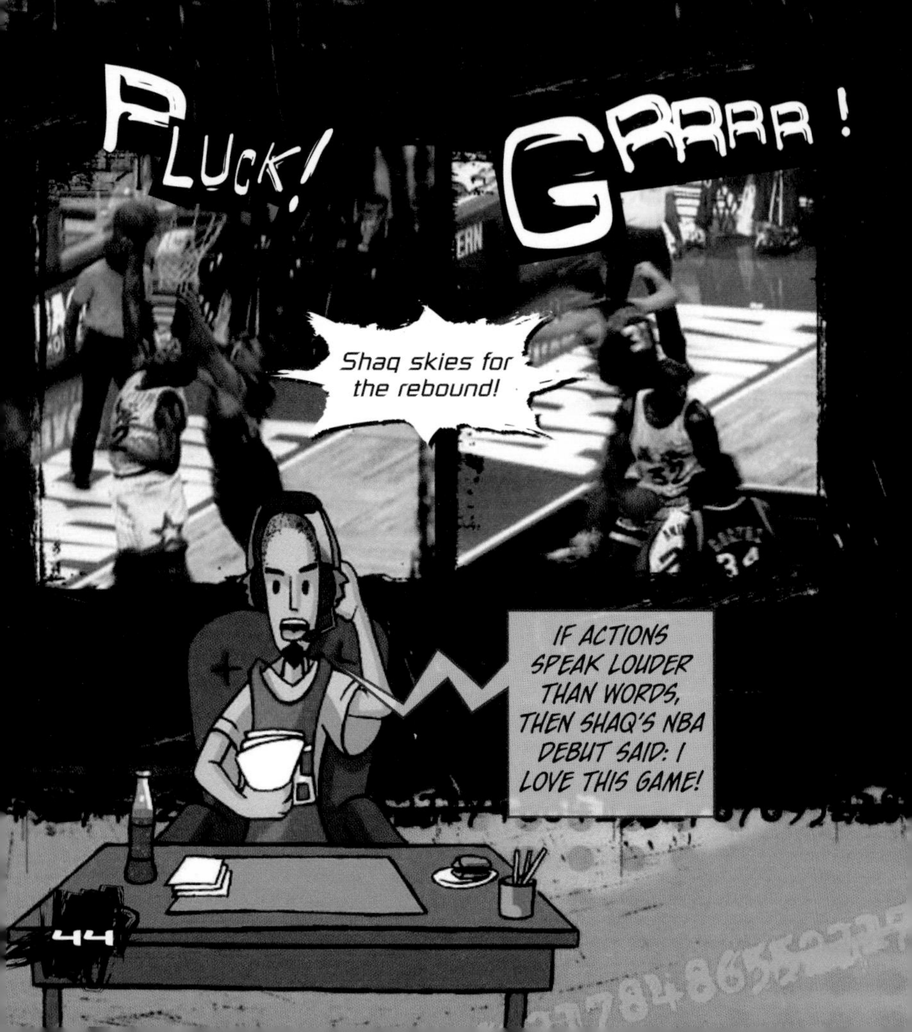
PLUCK!
GRRRRR!
Shaq skies for the rebound!
IF ACTIONS SPEAK LOUDER THAN WORDS, THEN SHAQ'S NBA DEBUT SAID: I LOVE THIS GAME!

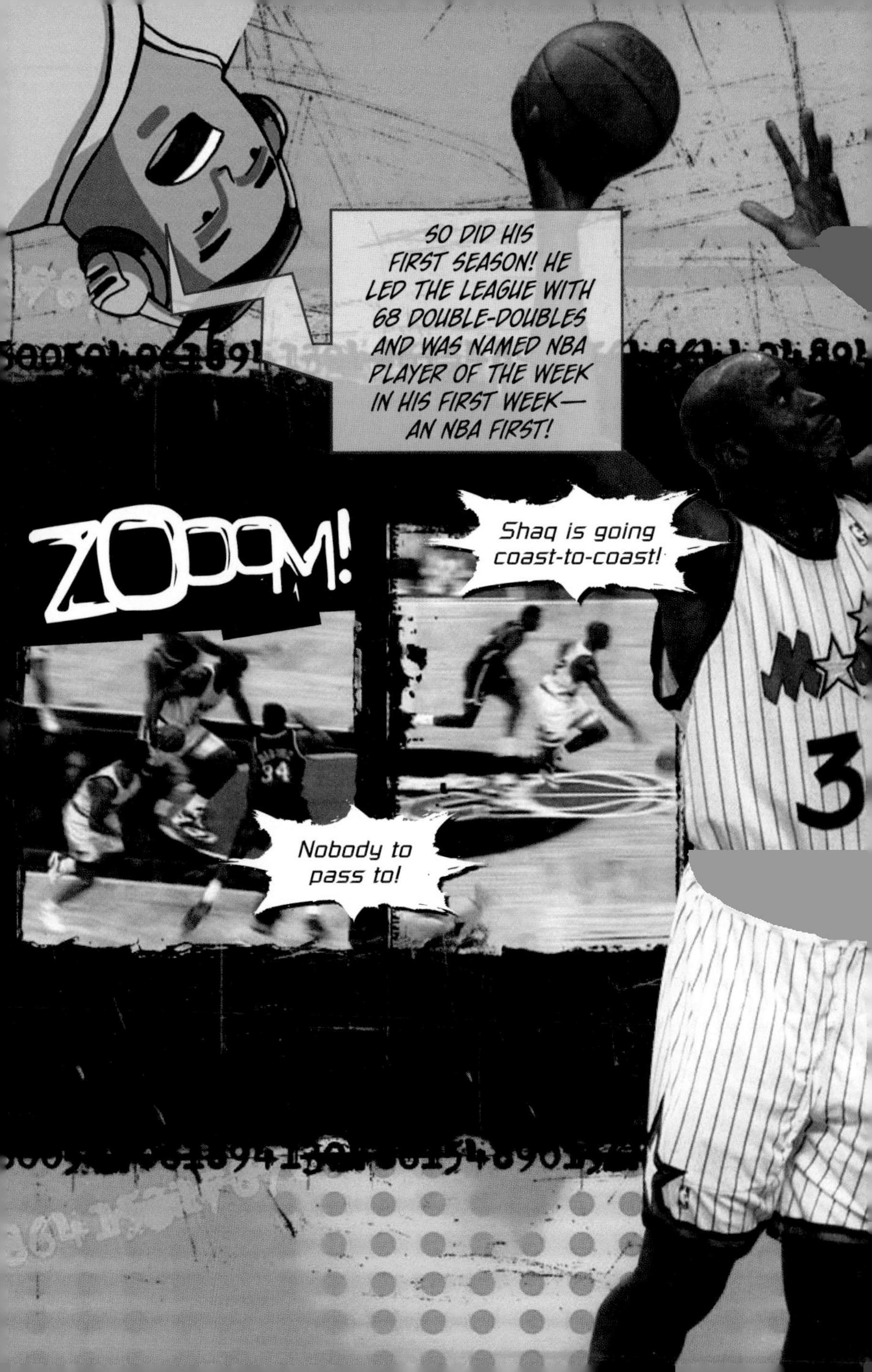
SO DID HIS FIRST SEASON! HE LED THE LEAGUE WITH 68 DOUBLE-DOUBLES AND WAS NAMED NBA PLAYER OF THE WEEK IN HIS FIRST WEEK— AN NBA FIRST!
ZOOOOM!
Shaq is going coast-to-coast!
Nobody to pass to!

April 13, 1997: Shaq Beats Utah at Buzzer!

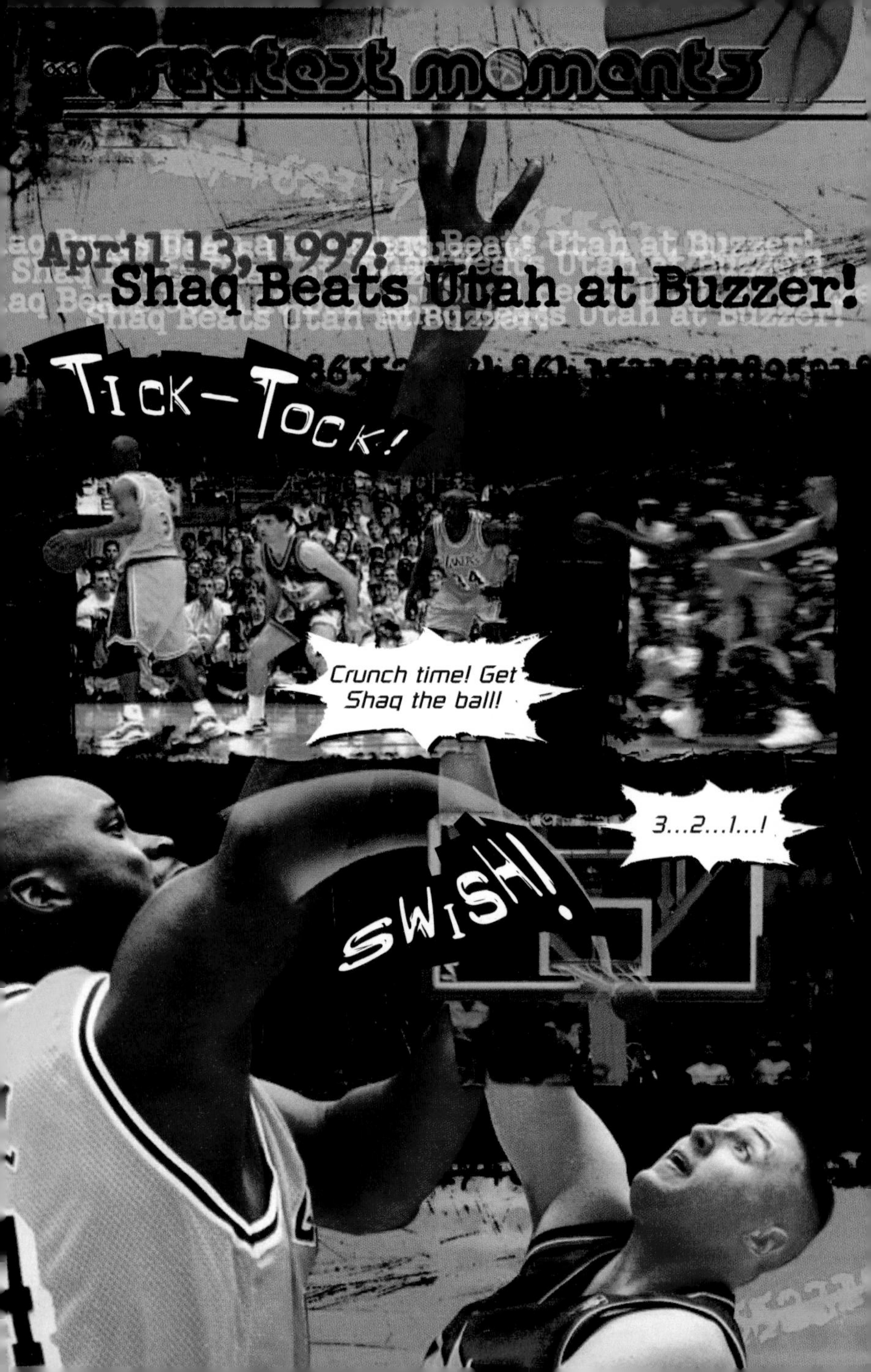
TICK-TOCK!
Crunch time! Get Shaq the ball!
3...2...1...!
SWISH!

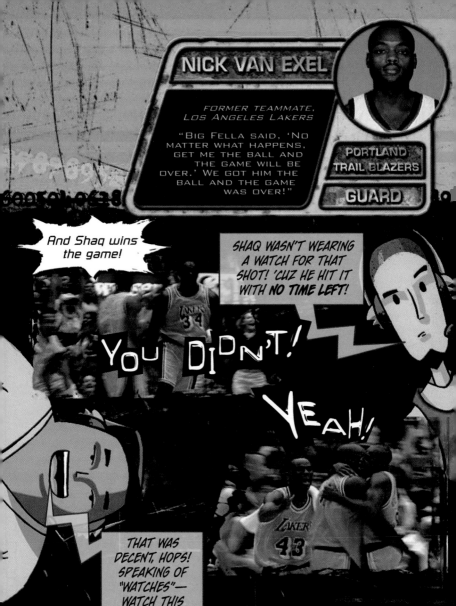

NICK VAN EXEL

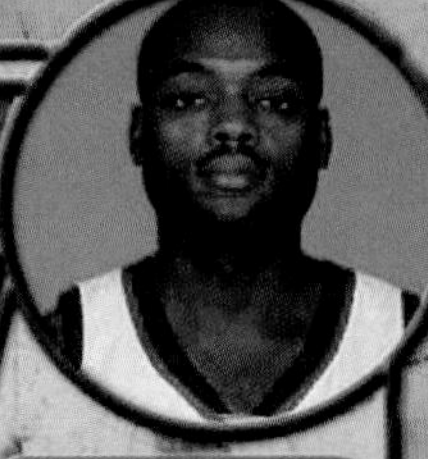

FORMER TEAMMATE, LOS ANGELES LAKERS

"BIG FELLA SAID, 'NO MATTER WHAT HAPPENS, GET ME THE BALL AND THE GAME WILL BE OVER.' WE GOT HIM THE BALL AND THE GAME WAS OVER!"

PORTLAND TRAIL BLAZERS

GUARD

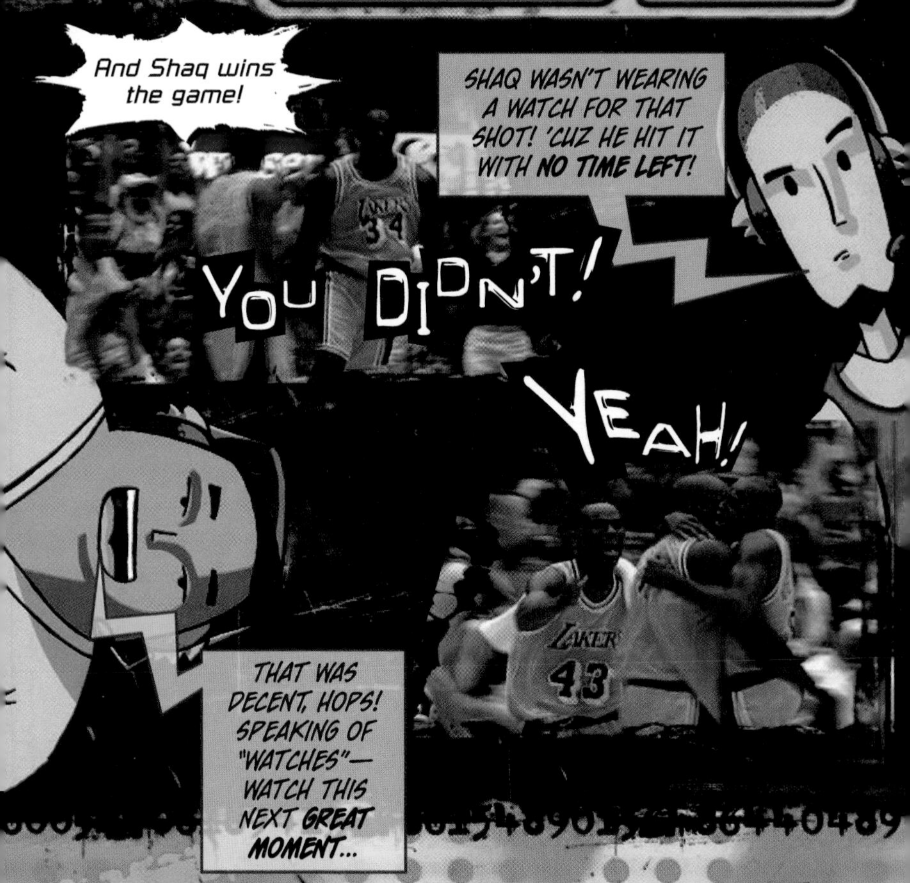
And Shaq wins the game!
SHAQ WASN'T WEARING A WATCH FOR THAT SHOT! 'CUZ HE HIT IT WITH NO TIME LEFT!
YOU DIDN'T!
YEAH!
THAT WAS DECENT, HOPS! SPEAKING OF "WATCHES"— WATCH THIS NEXT GREAT MOMENT...

May 9, 1999: Shaq Stuffs Rockets in Game 1 of NBA Playoffs!

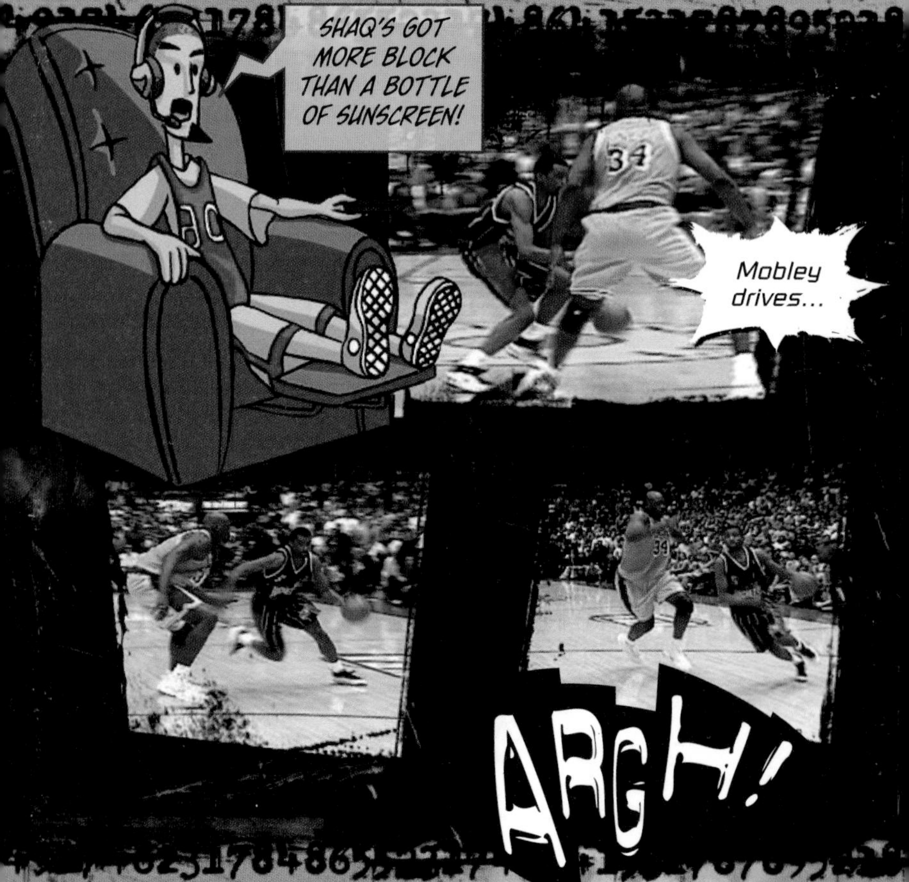
SHAQ'S GOT MORE BLOCK THAN A BOTTLE OF SUNSCREEN!
Mobley drives...
ARGH!

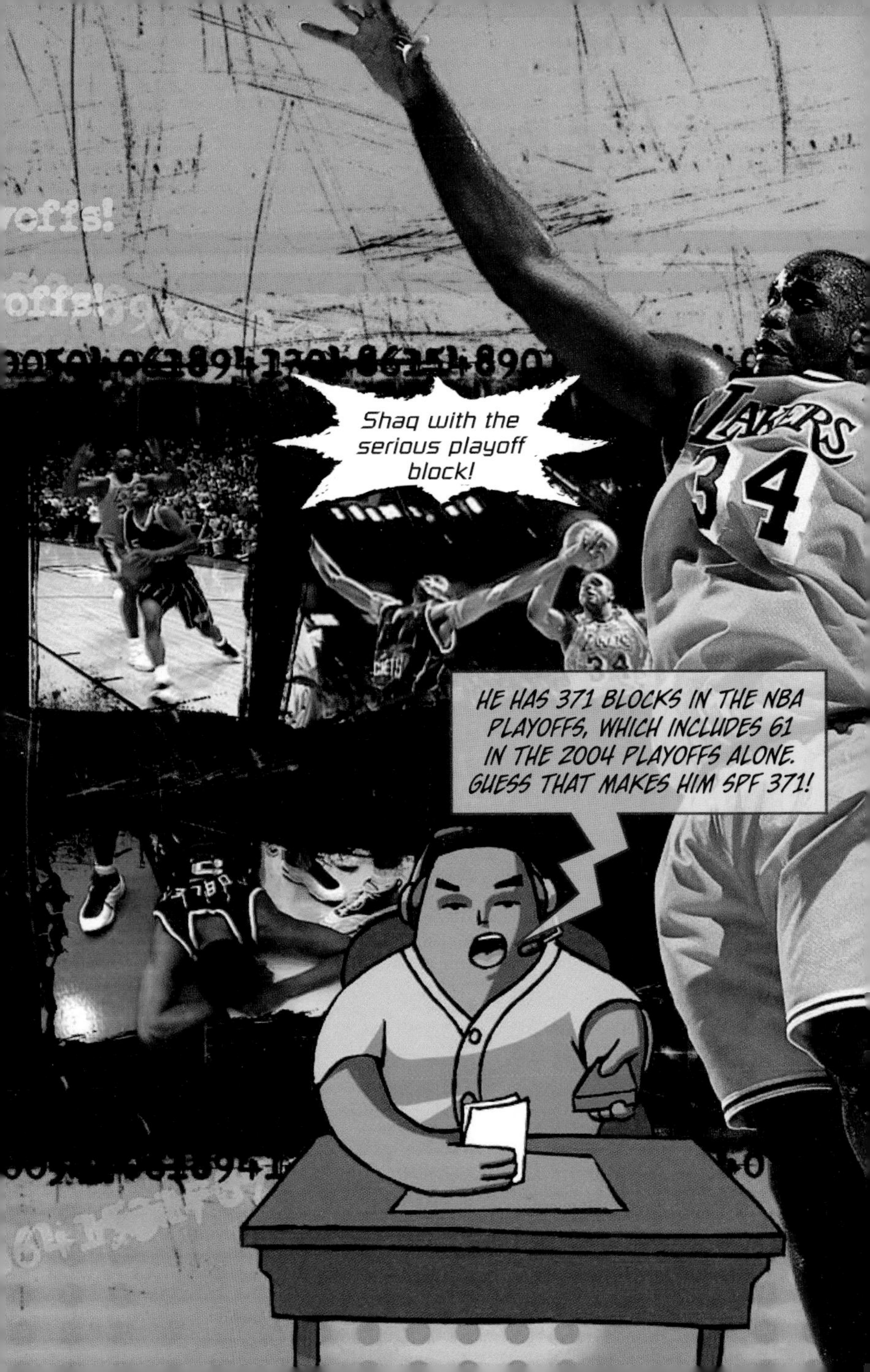
Shaq with the serious playoff block!
HE HAS 371 BLOCKS IN THE NBA PLAYOFFS, WHICH INCLUDES 61 IN THE 2004 PLAYOFFS ALONE. GUESS THAT MAKES HIM SPF 371!

May 1995:
Shaq Leads The Magic to the Eastern Conference Title

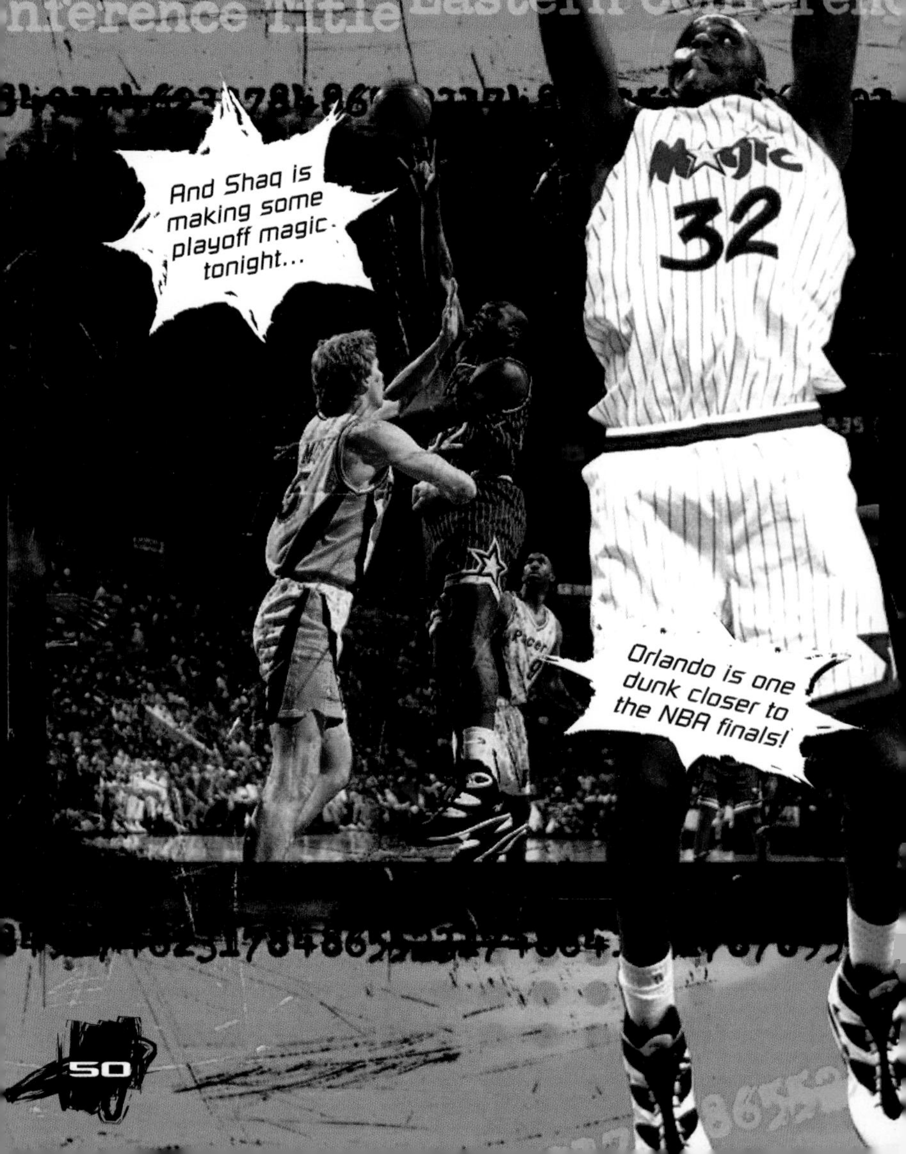
And Shaq is making some playoff magic tonight...
Orlando is one dunk closer to the NBA finals!

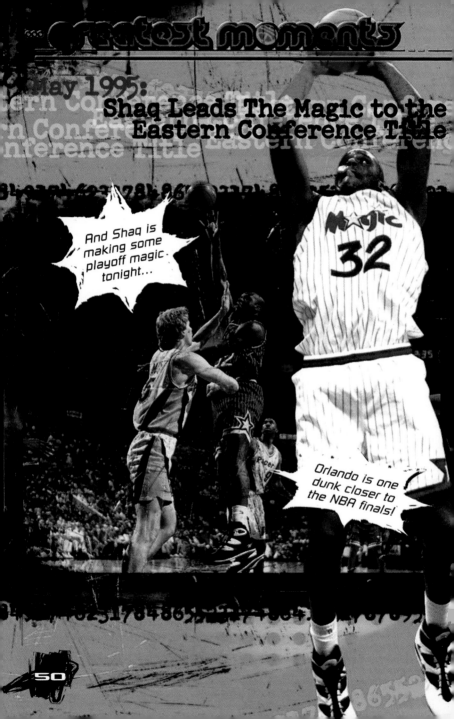

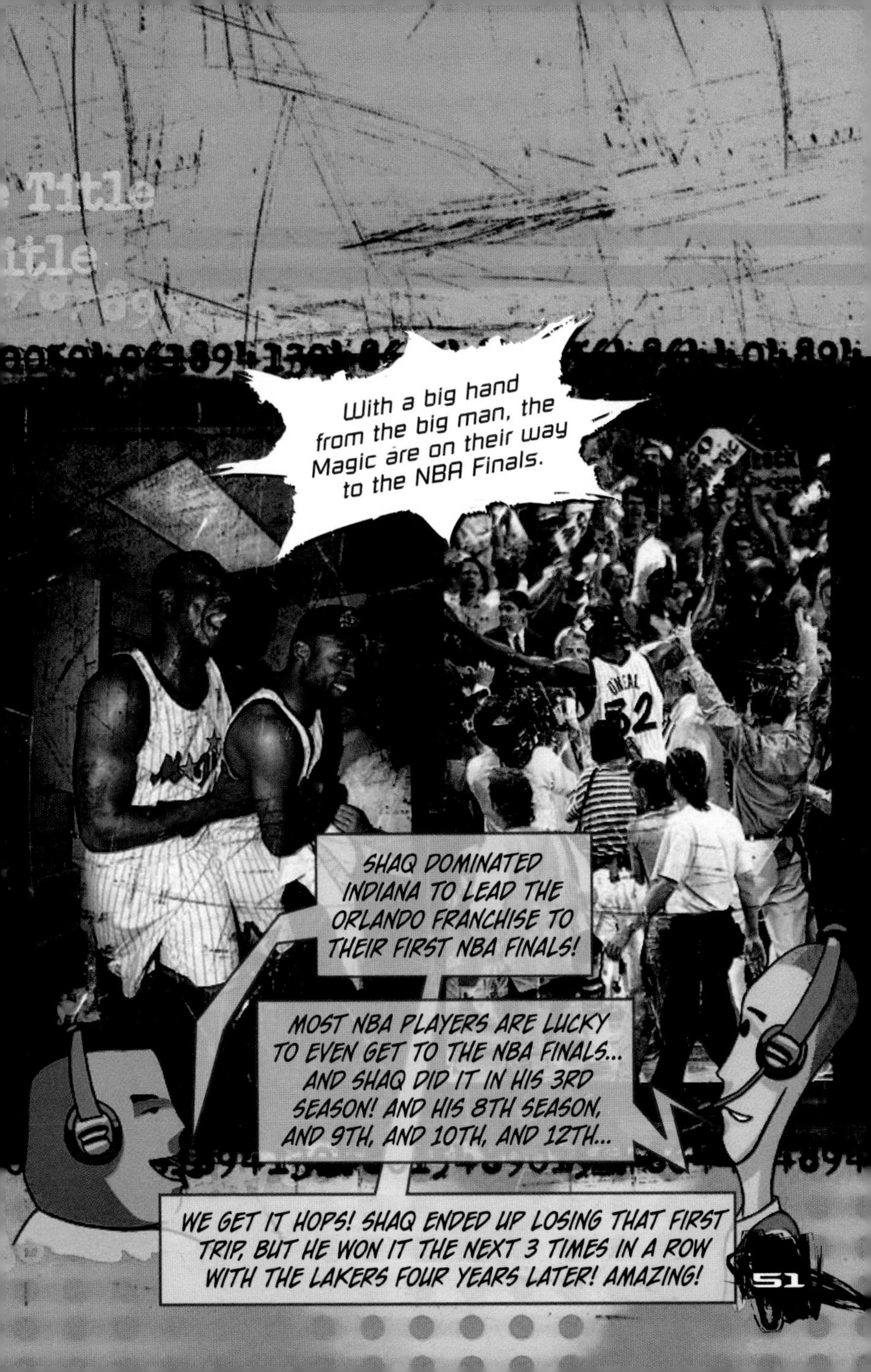
With a big hand from the big man, the Magic are on their way to the NBA Finals.
SHAQ DOMINATED INDIANA TO LEAD THE ORLANDO FRANCHISE TO THEIR FIRST NBA FINALS!
MOST NBA PLAYERS ARE LUCKY TO EVEN GET TO THE NBA FINALS... AND SHAQ DID IT IN HIS 3RD SEASON! AND HIS 8TH SEASON, AND 9TH, AND 10TH, AND 12TH...
WE GET IT HOPS! SHAQ ENDED UP LOSING THAT FIRST TRIP, BUT HE WON IT THE NEXT 3 TIMES IN A ROW WITH THE LAKERS FOUR YEARS LATER! AMAZING!

March 6, 2000: Shaq Scores 61 on His 28th Birthday

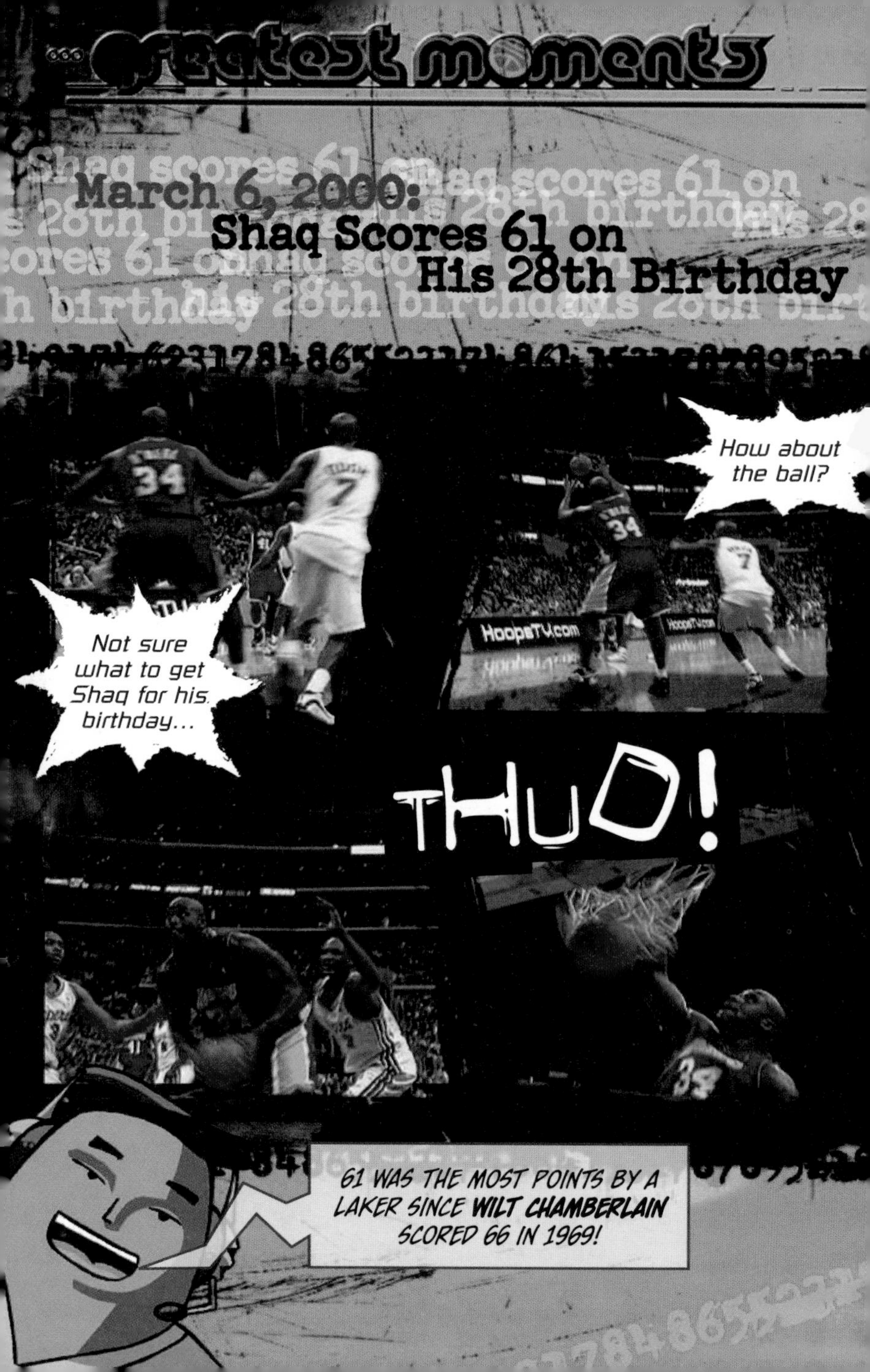
Not sure what to get Shaq for his birthday...
How about the ball?
THUD!
61 WAS THE MOST POINTS BY A LAKER SINCE **WILT CHAMBERLAIN** SCORED 66 IN 1969!

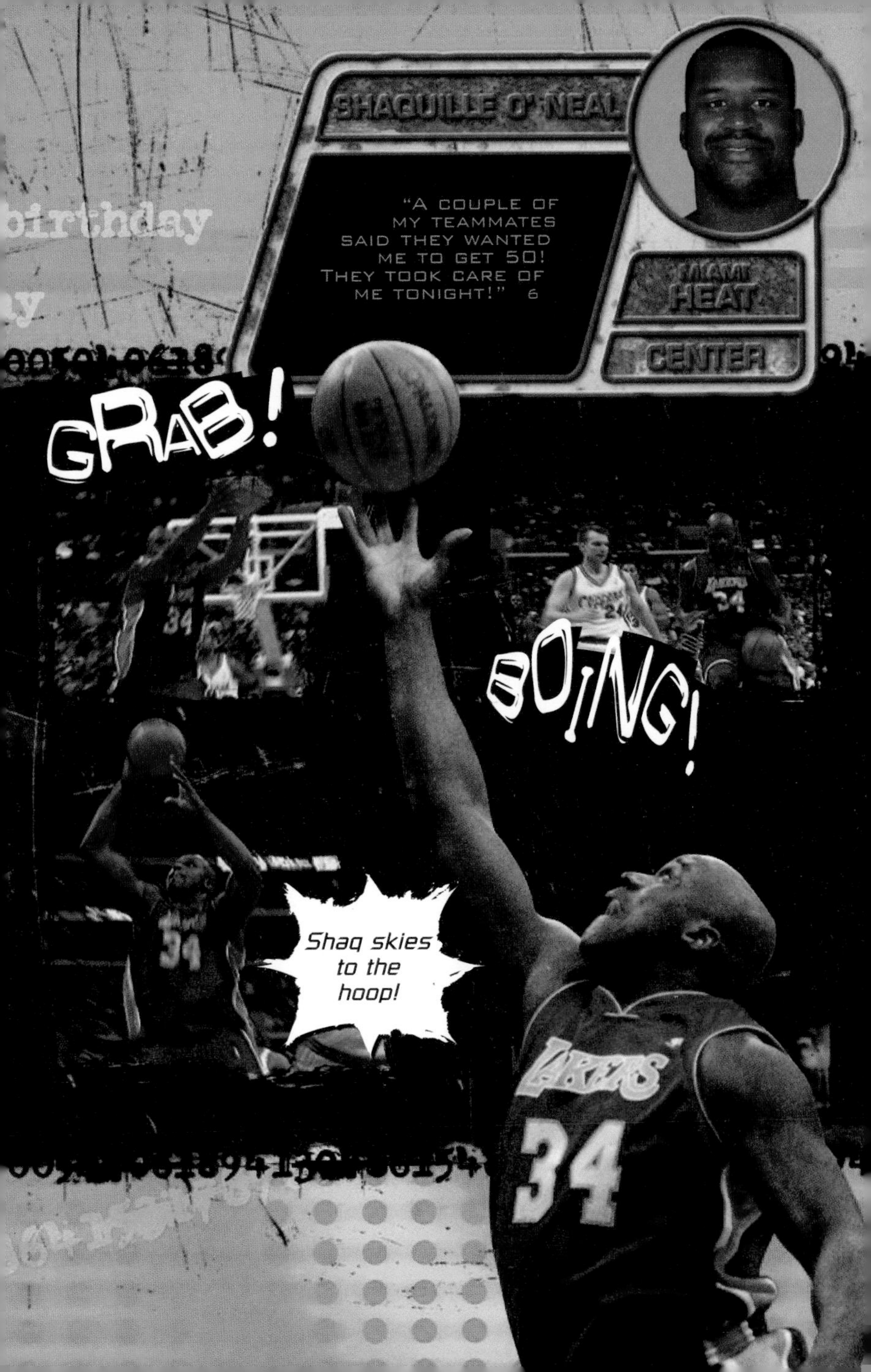
SHAQUILLE O'NEAL
"A COUPLE OF MY TEAMMATES SAID THEY WANTED ME TO GET 50! THEY TOOK CARE OF ME TONIGHT!" 6
HEAT
CENTER
GRAB!
BOING!
Shaq skies to the hoop!

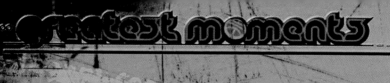

March 26, 2000: Shaq Wins the Game at Both Ends vs. Kings

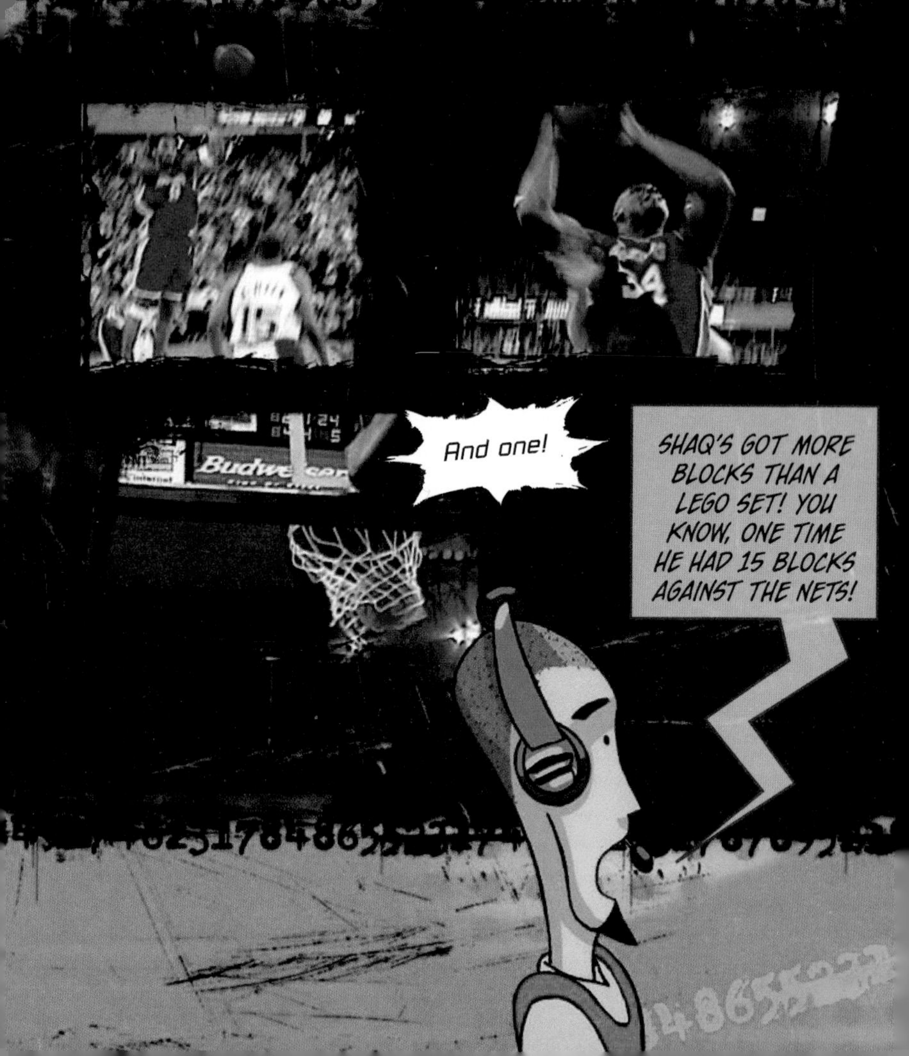
And one!
SHAQ'S GOT MORE BLOCKS THAN A LEGO SET! YOU KNOW, ONE TIME HE HAD 15 BLOCKS AGAINST THE NETS!

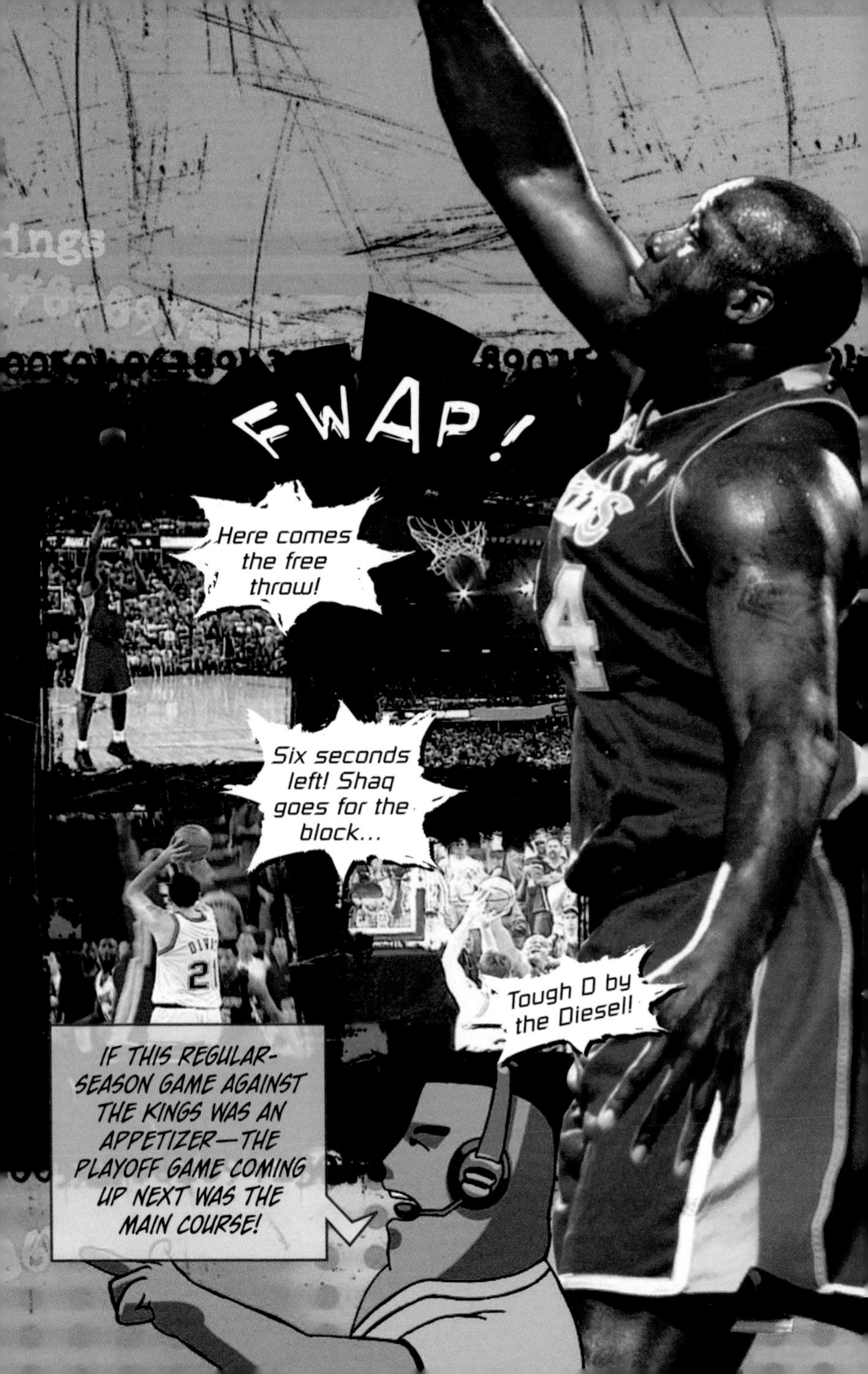
FWAP!
Here comes the free throw!
Six seconds left! Shaq goes for the block...
Tough D by the Diesel!
IF THIS REGULAR-SEASON GAME AGAINST THE KINGS WAS AN APPETIZER—THE PLAYOFF GAME COMING UP NEXT WAS THE MAIN COURSE!

April 23, 2000:
Shaq Drops 46 Against Kings in NBA Playoffs!

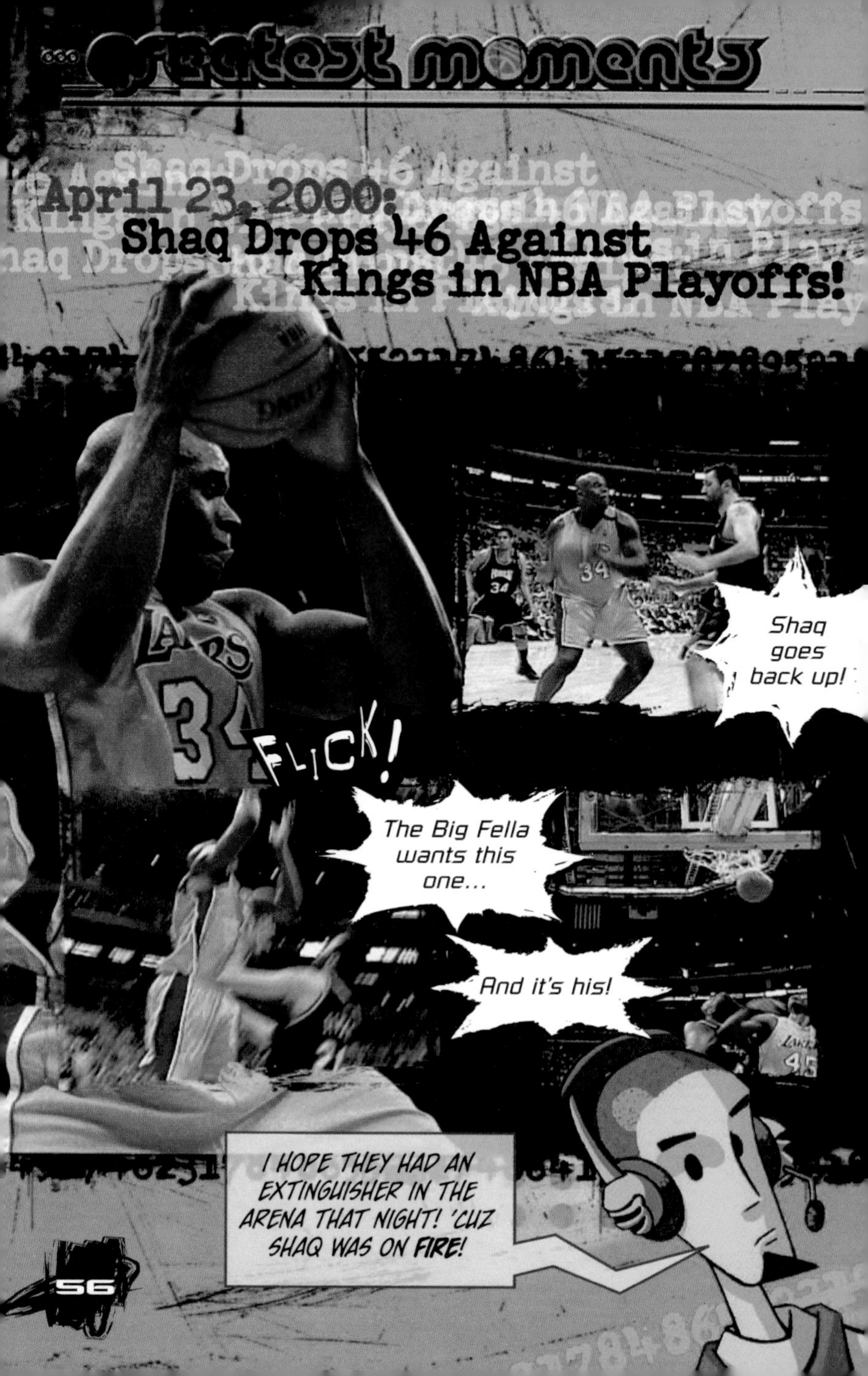
Shaq goes back up!
FLICK!
The Big Fella wants this one...
And it's his!
I HOPE THEY HAD AN EXTINGUISHER IN THE ARENA THAT NIGHT! 'CUZ SHAQ WAS ON FIRE!

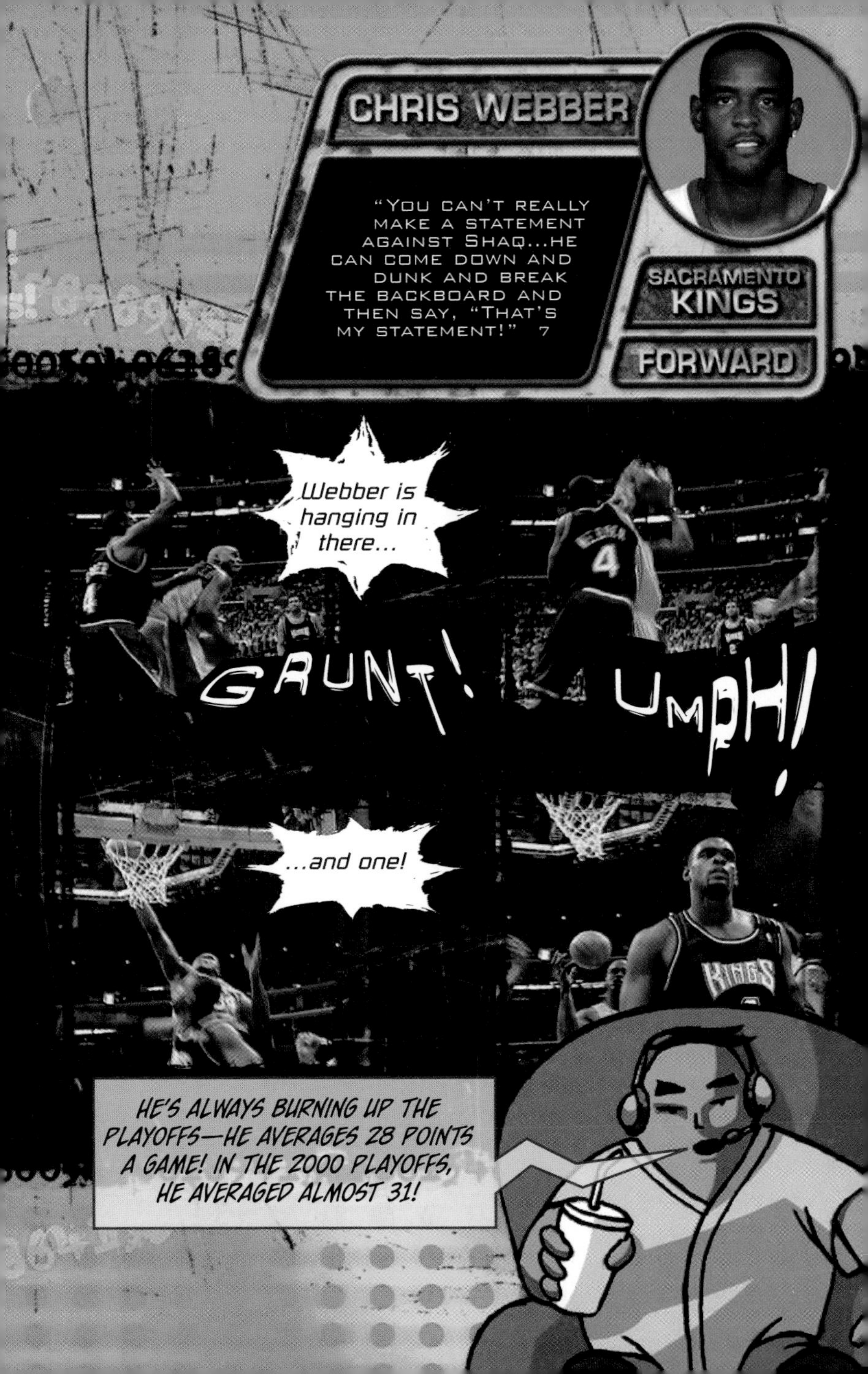
CHRIS WEBBER
"YOU CAN'T REALLY MAKE A STATEMENT AGAINST SHAQ...HE CAN COME DOWN AND DUNK AND BREAK THE BACKBOARD AND THEN SAY, "THAT'S MY STATEMENT!" [7]
SACRAMENTO KINGS
FORWARD
Webber is hanging in there...
GRUNT!
UMPH!
...and one!
HE'S ALWAYS BURNING UP THE PLAYOFFS—HE AVERAGES 28 POINTS A GAME! IN THE 2000 PLAYOFFS, HE AVERAGED ALMOST 31!

May 28, 2000: 9 for 9 From the Stripe vs. Portland in the Playoffs!

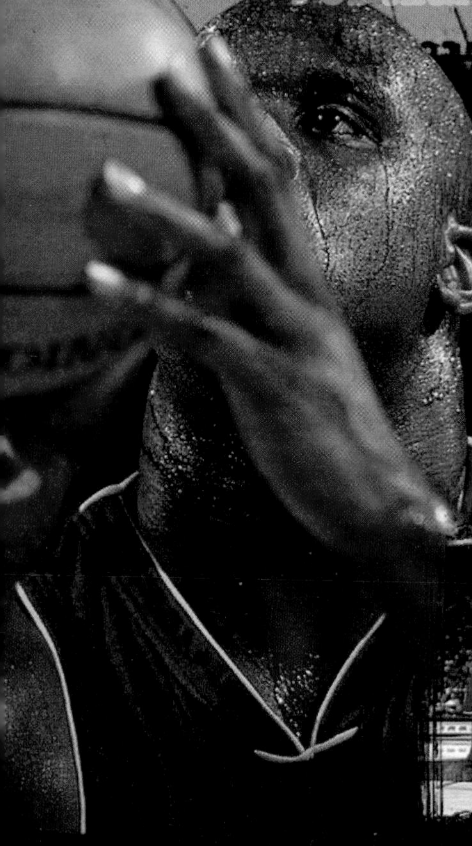

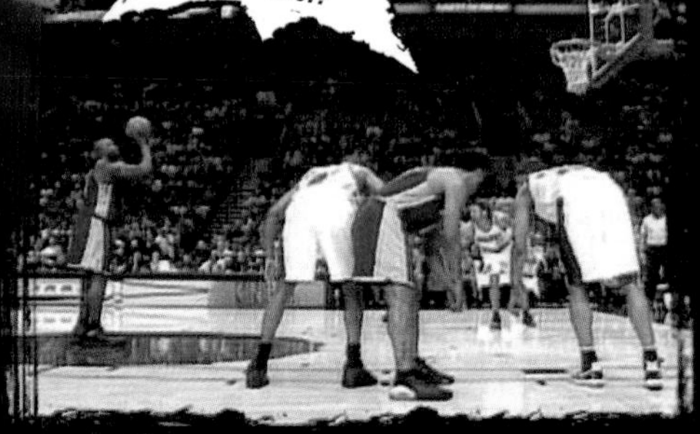
Shaq focuses... Snaps his wrist!!

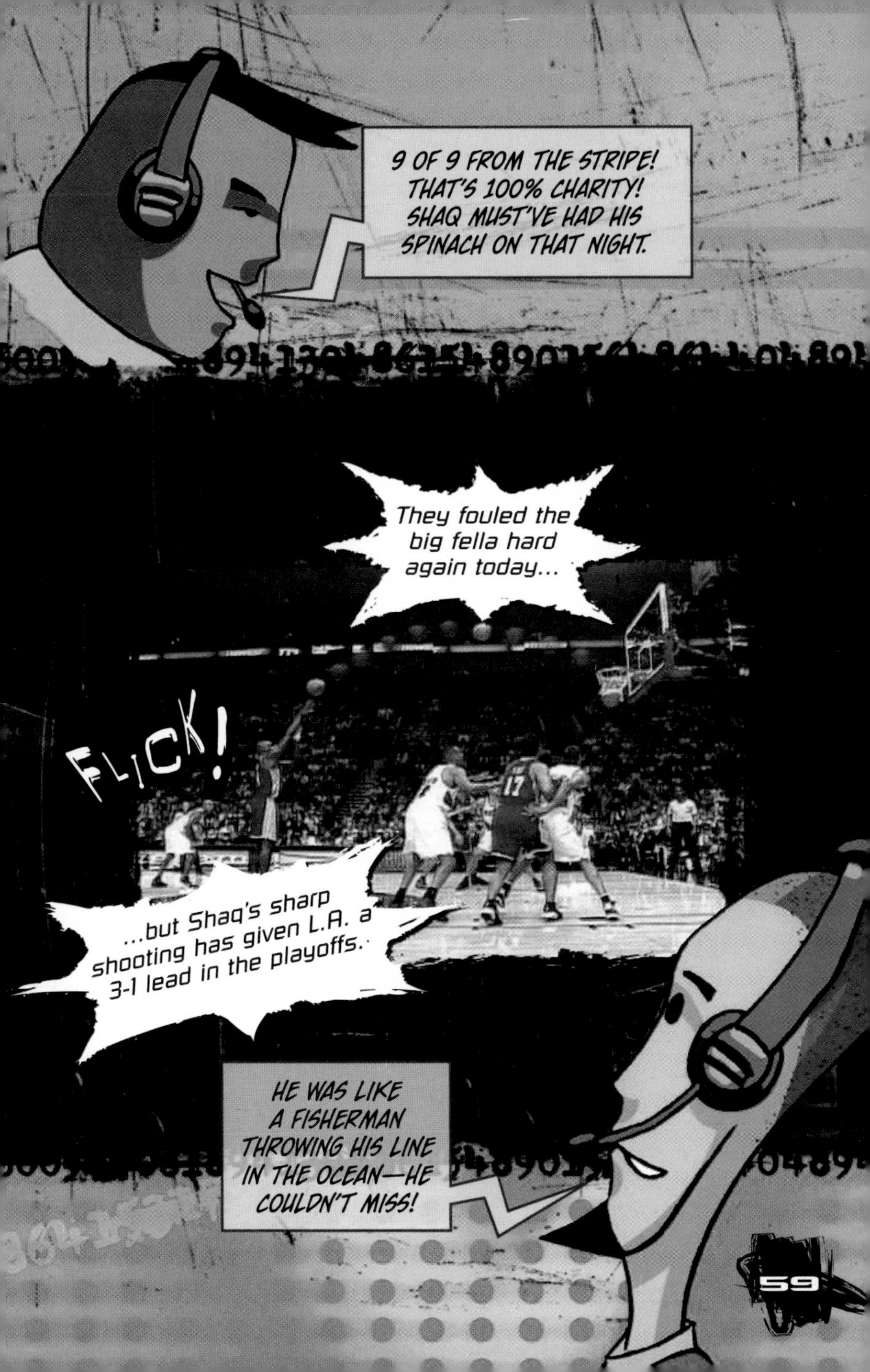
9 OF 9 FROM THE STRIPE! THAT'S 100% CHARITY! SHAQ MUST'VE HAD HIS SPINACH ON THAT NIGHT.
They fouled the big fella hard again today...
FLICK!
...but Shaq's sharp shooting has given L.A. a 3-1 lead in the playoffs.
HE WAS LIKE A FISHERMAN THROWING HIS LINE IN THE OCEAN—HE COULDN'T MISS!

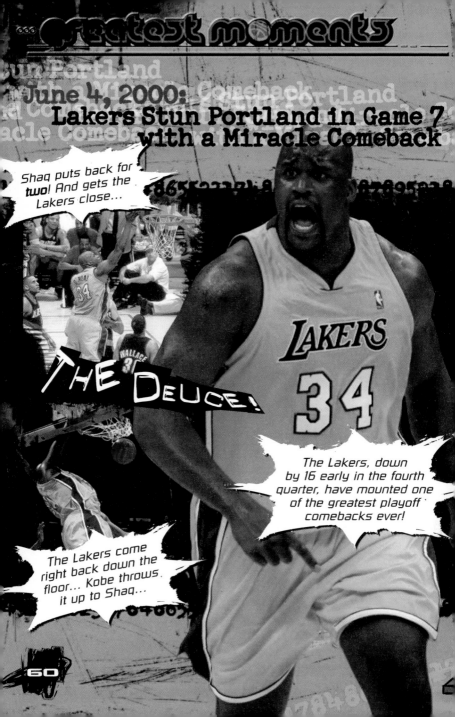

June 4, 2000: Lakers Stun Portland in Game 7 with a Miracle Comeback

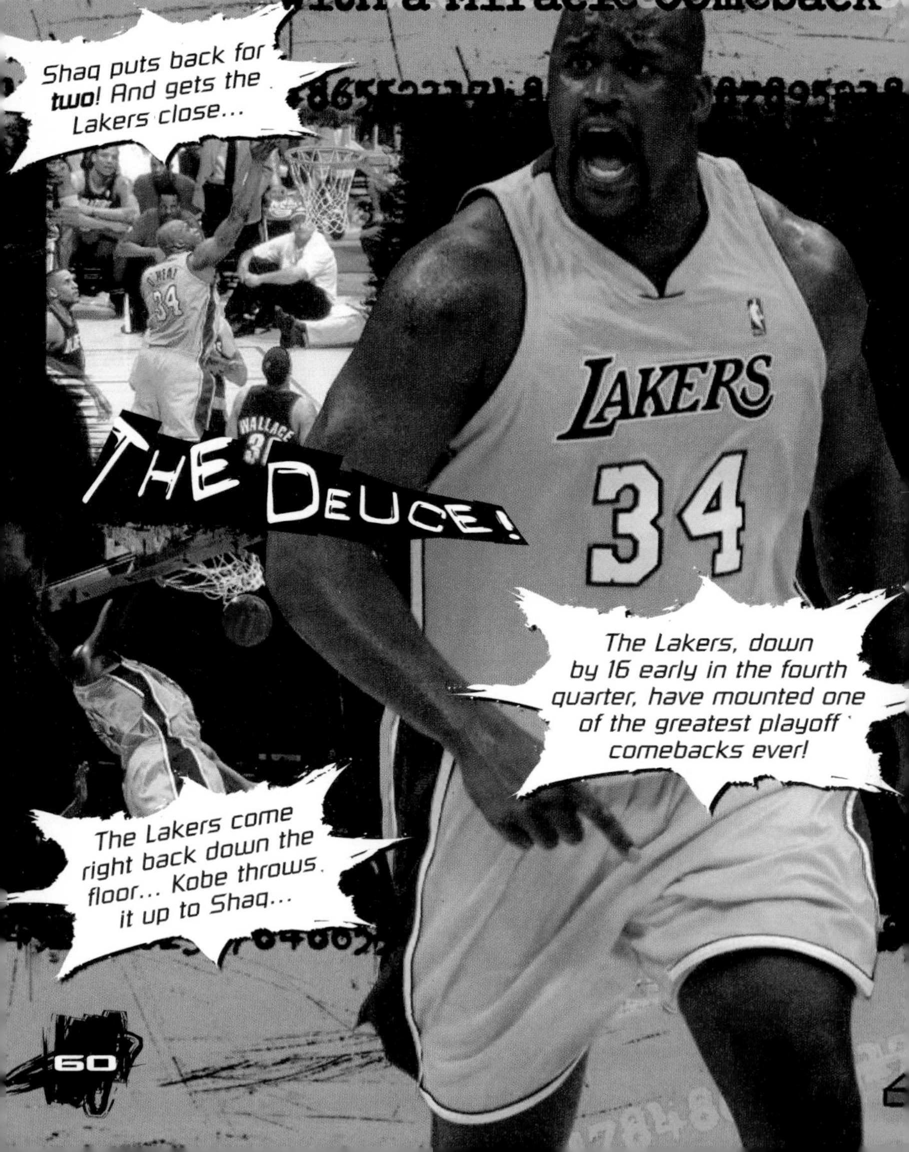
Shaq puts back for **two**! And gets the Lakers close...
THE DEUCE!
LAKERS
34
The Lakers, down by 16 early in the fourth quarter, have mounted one of the greatest playoff comebacks ever!
The Lakers come right back down the floor... Kobe throws it up to Shaq...

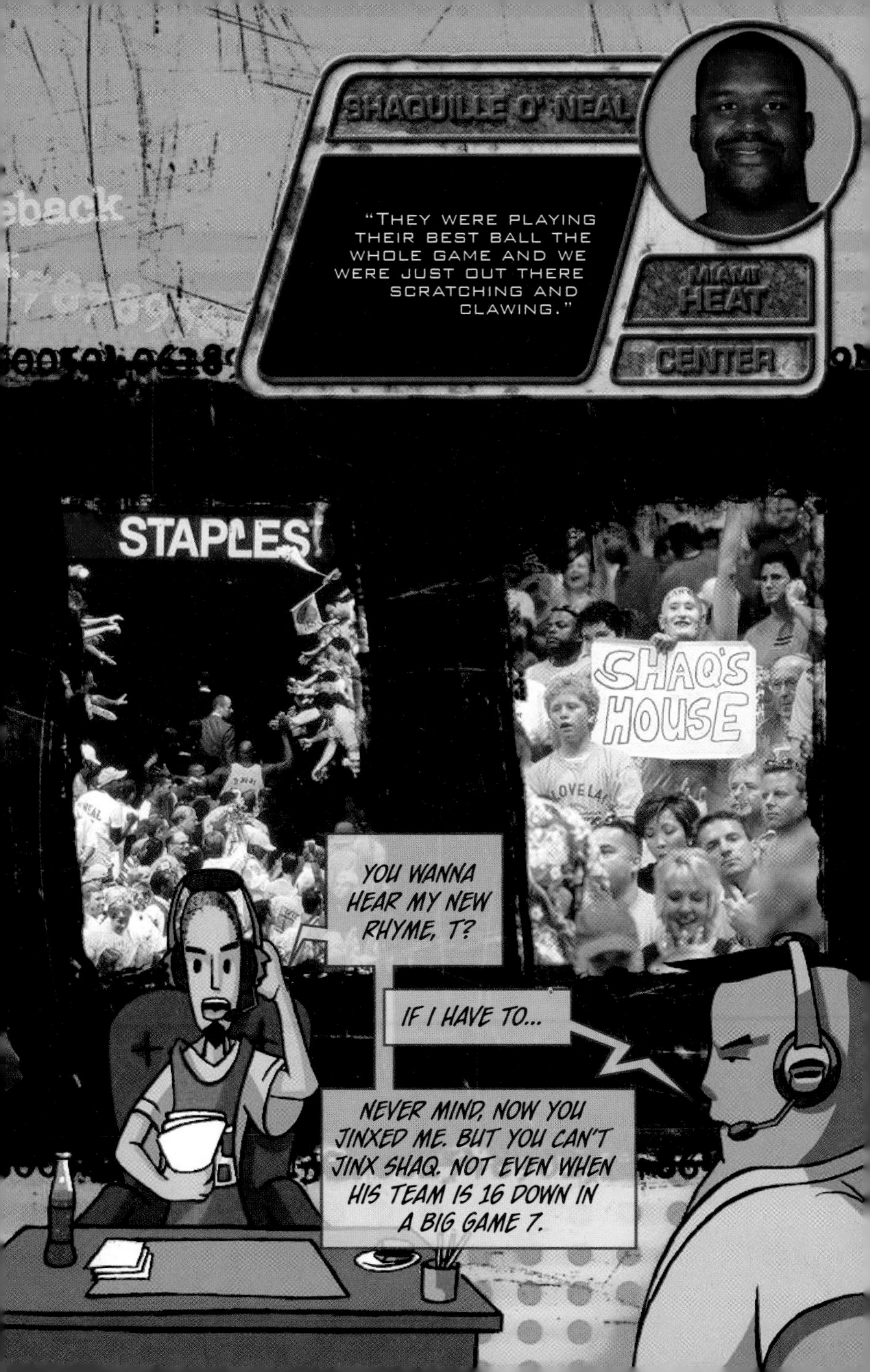
SHAQUILLE O' NEAL
"THEY WERE PLAYING THEIR BEST BALL THE WHOLE GAME AND WE WERE JUST OUT THERE SCRATCHING AND CLAWING."
MIAMI HEAT
CENTER
STAPLES
SHAQ'S HOUSE
YOU WANNA HEAR MY NEW RHYME, T?
IF I HAVE TO...
NEVER MIND, NOW YOU JINXED ME. BUT YOU CAN'T JINX SHAQ. NOT EVEN WHEN HIS TEAM IS 16 DOWN IN A BIG GAME 7.

March 21, 2003: Shaq Crushes Celtics with 48 Points and 20 Rebounds!

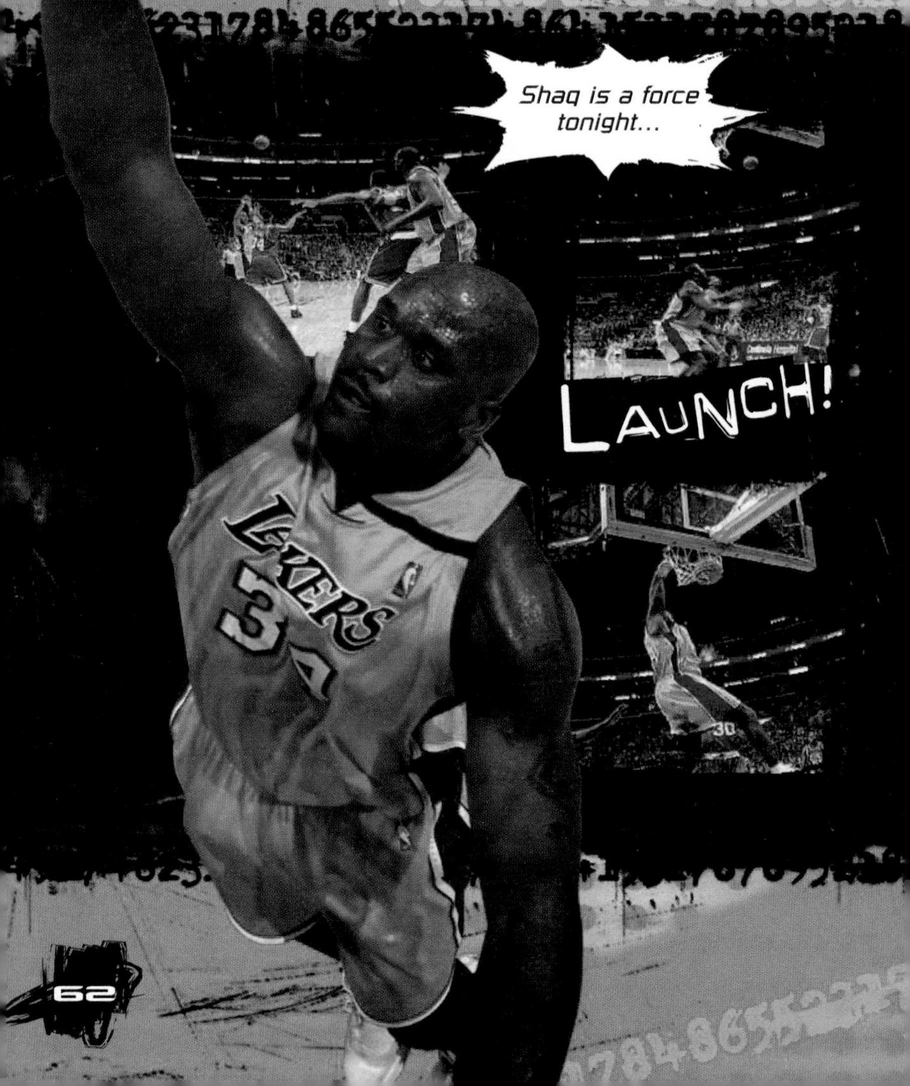

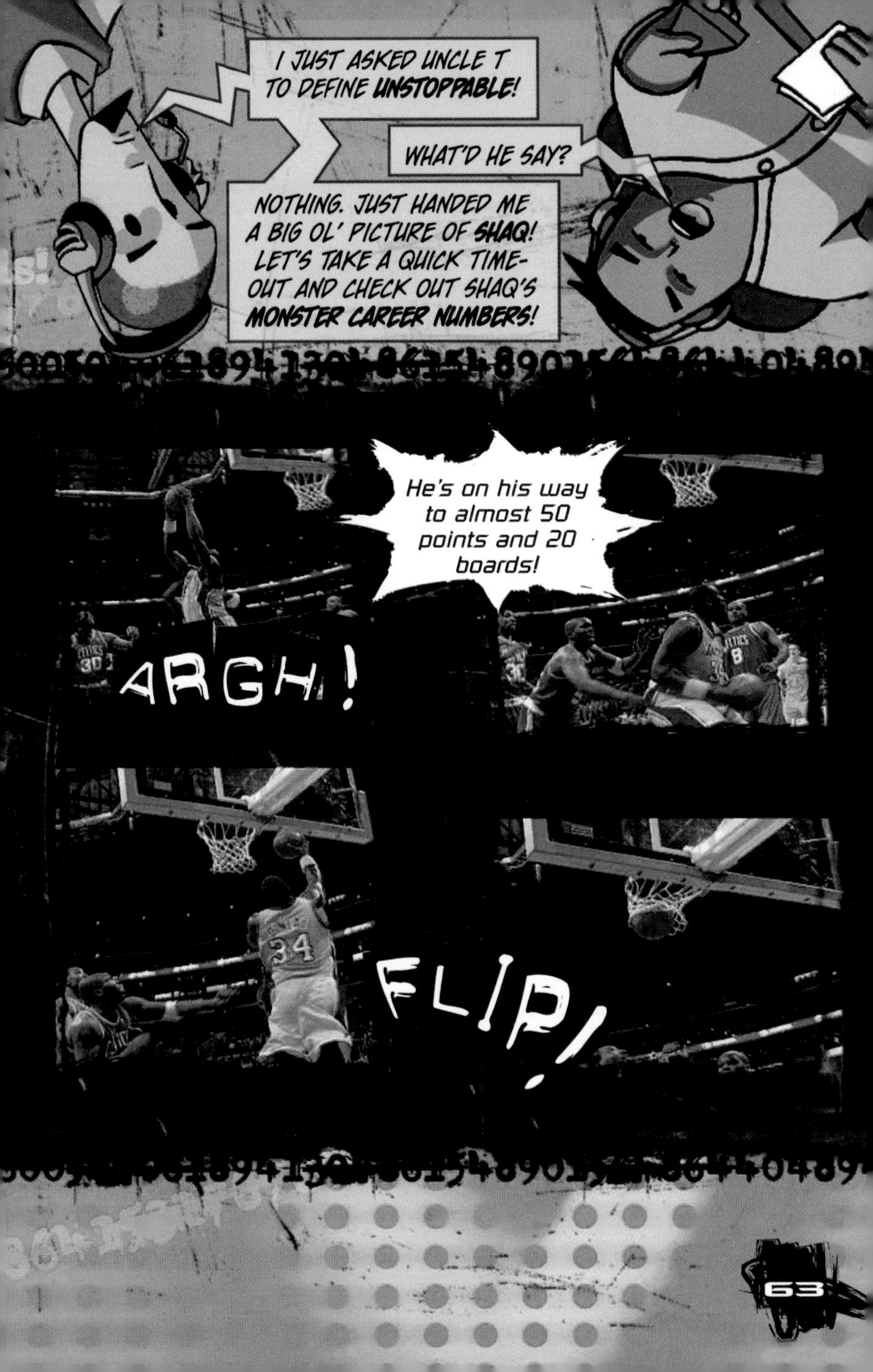

I JUST ASKED UNCLE T TO DEFINE UNSTOPPABLE!
WHAT'D HE SAY?
NOTHING. JUST HANDED ME A BIG OL' PICTURE OF SHAQ! LET'S TAKE A QUICK TIME-OUT AND CHECK OUT SHAQ'S MONSTER CAREER NUMBERS!
He's on his way to almost 50 points and 20 boards!
ARGH!
FLIP!

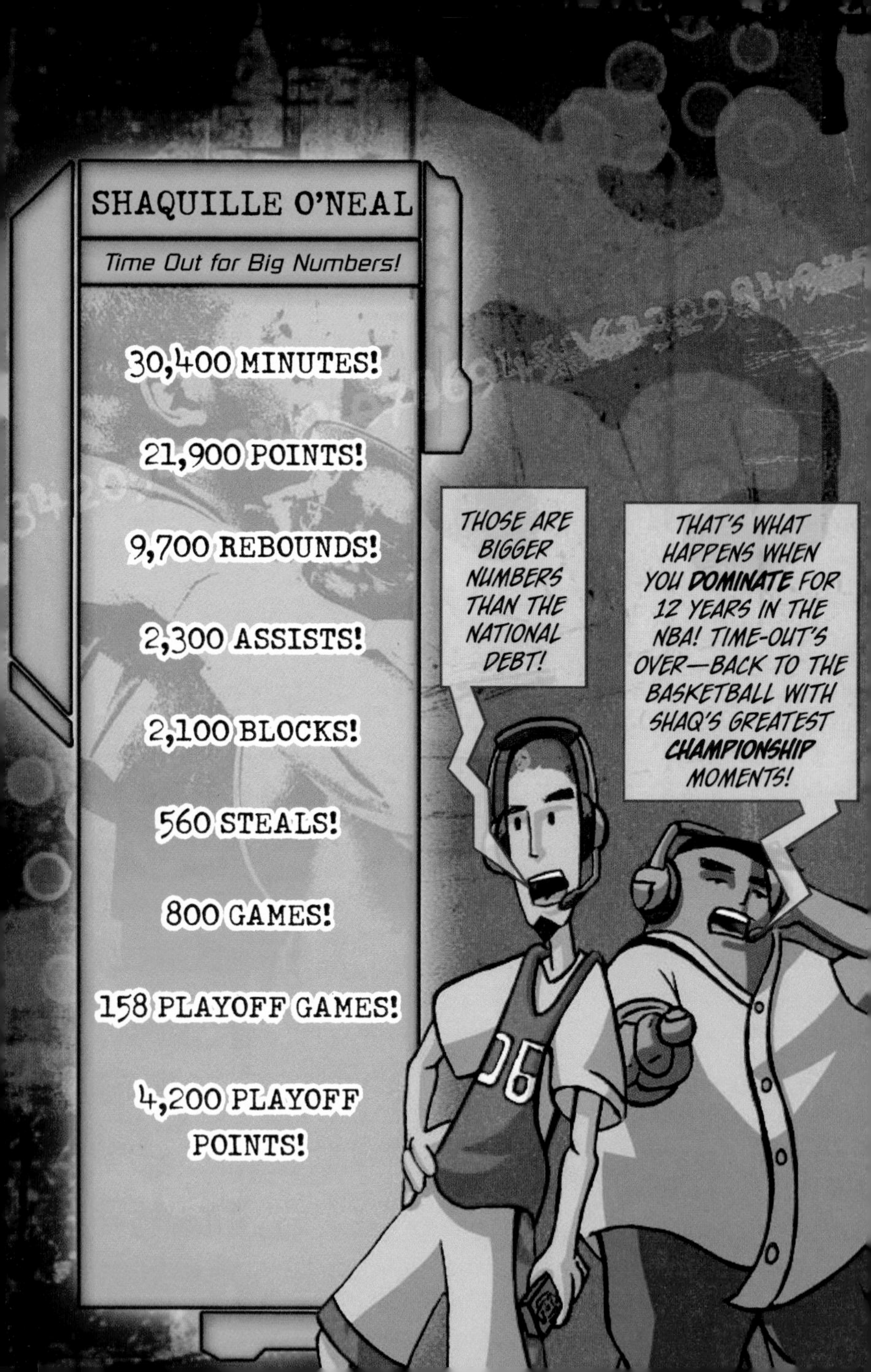
SHAQUILLE O'NEAL
Time Out for Big Numbers!
30,400 MINUTES!
21,900 POINTS!
9,700 REBOUNDS!
2,300 ASSISTS!
2,100 BLOCKS!
560 STEALS!
800 GAMES!
158 PLAYOFF GAMES!
4,200 PLAYOFF POINTS!
THOSE ARE BIGGER NUMBERS THAN THE NATIONAL DEBT!
THAT'S WHAT HAPPENS WHEN YOU **DOMINATE** FOR 12 YEARS IN THE NBA! TIME-OUT'S OVER—BACK TO THE BASKETBALL WITH SHAQ'S GREATEST **CHAMPIONSHIP** MOMENTS!

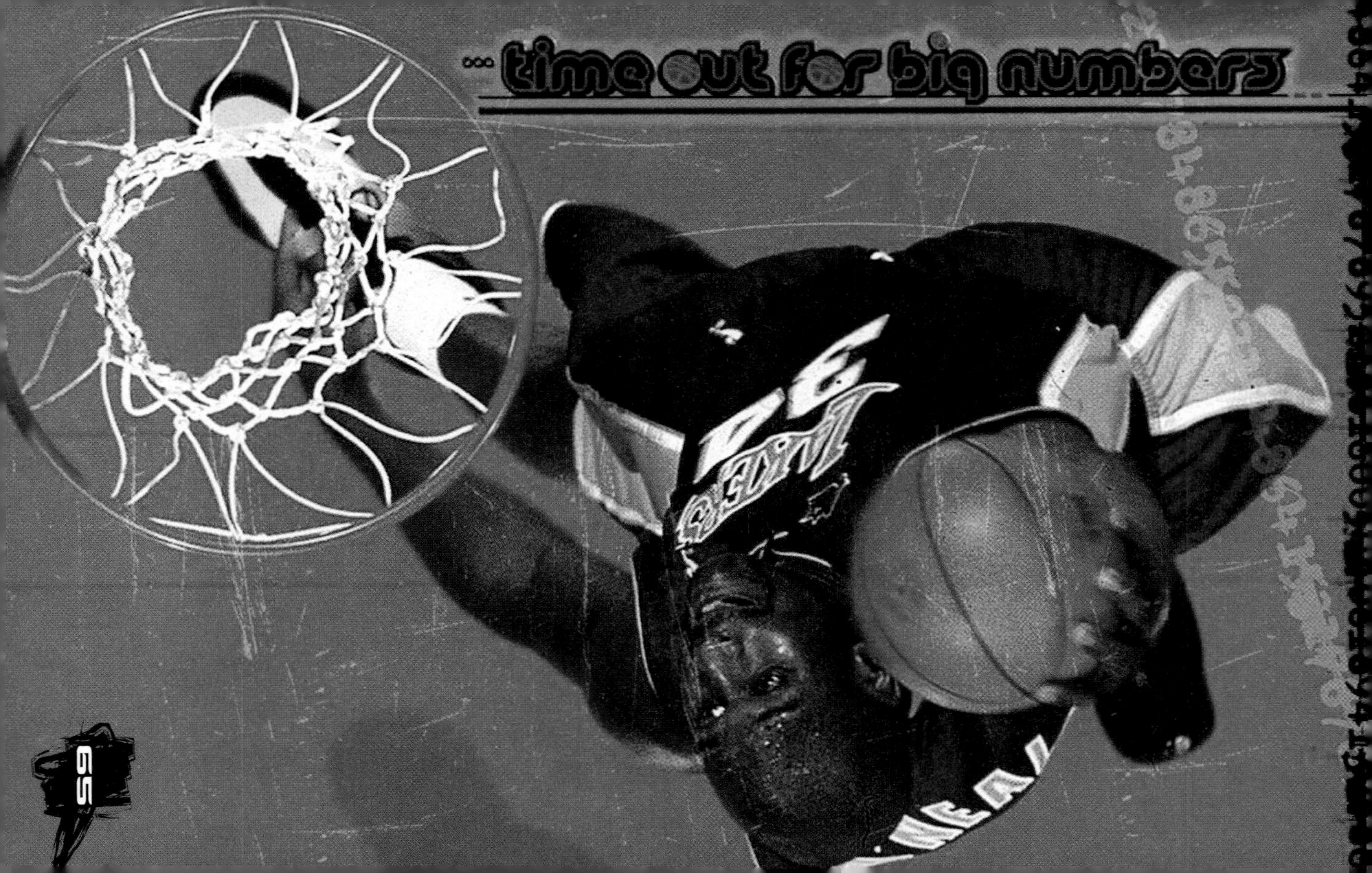

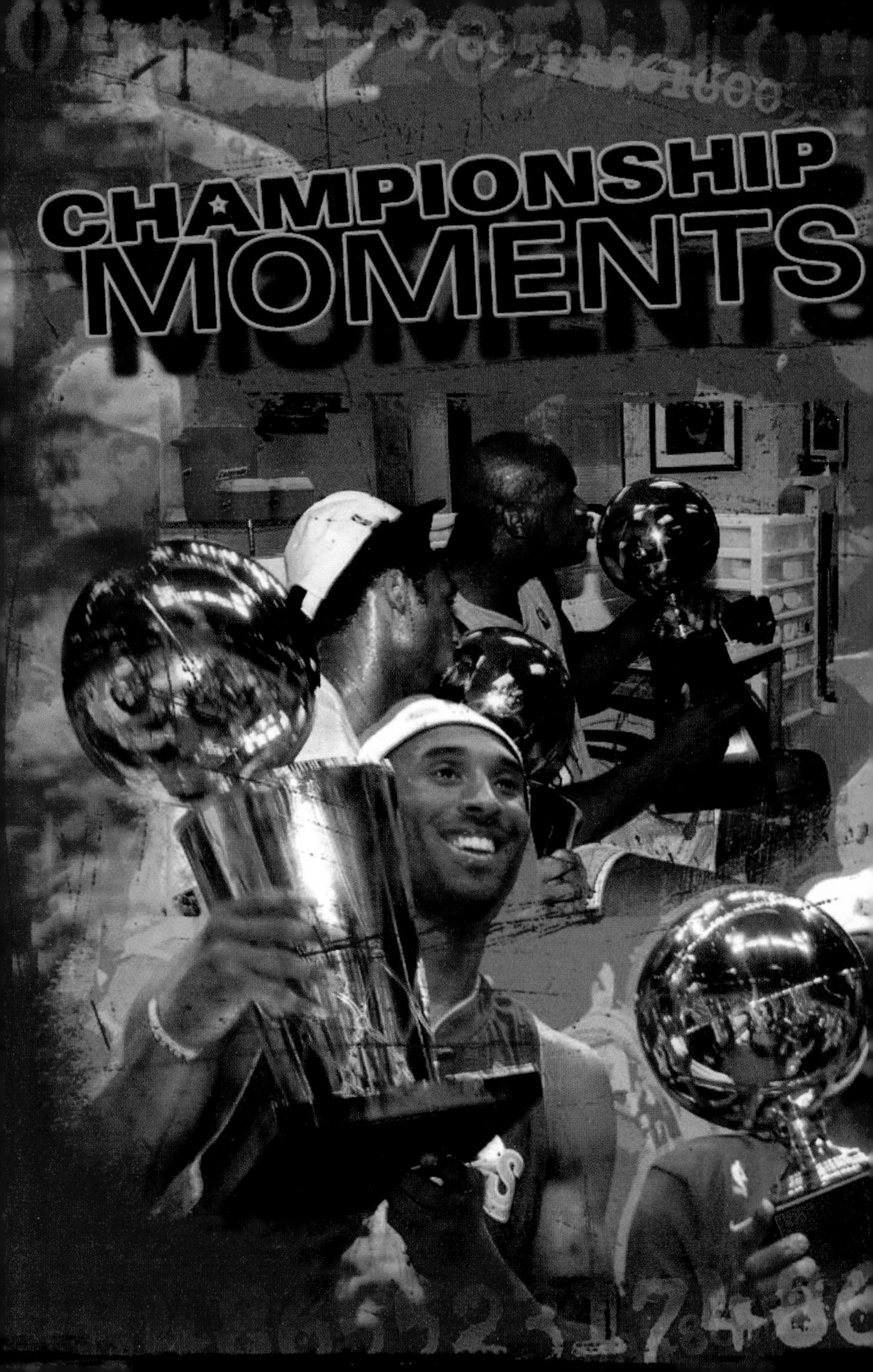
CHAMPIONSHIP
MOMENTS

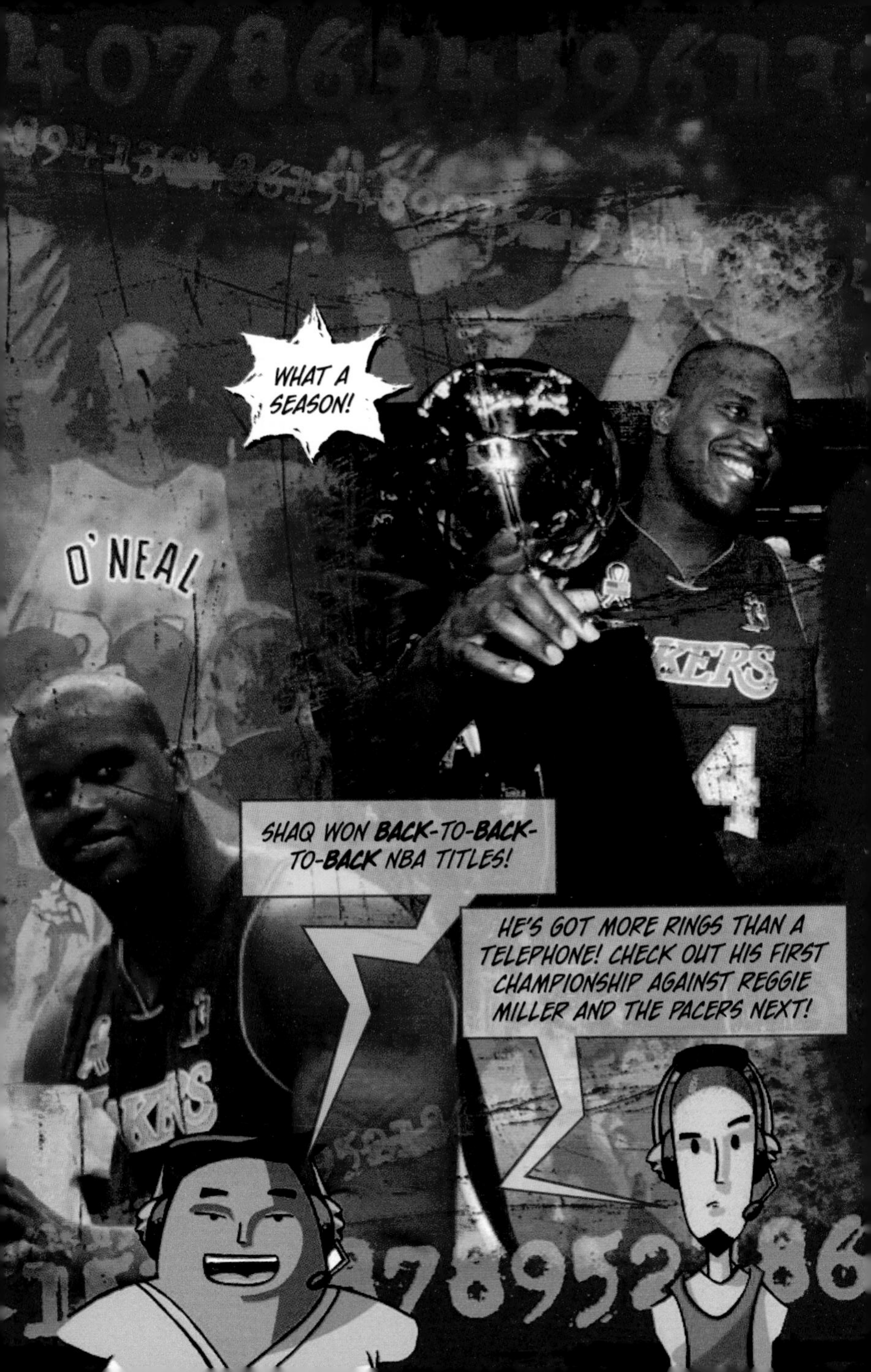
WHAT A SEASON!
O'NEAL
SHAQ WON BACK-TO-BACK-TO-BACK NBA TITLES!
HE'S GOT MORE RINGS THAN A TELEPHONE! CHECK OUT HIS FIRST CHAMPIONSHIP AGAINST REGGIE MILLER AND THE PACERS NEXT!

June 2000:
First Championship (vs. Pacers)!

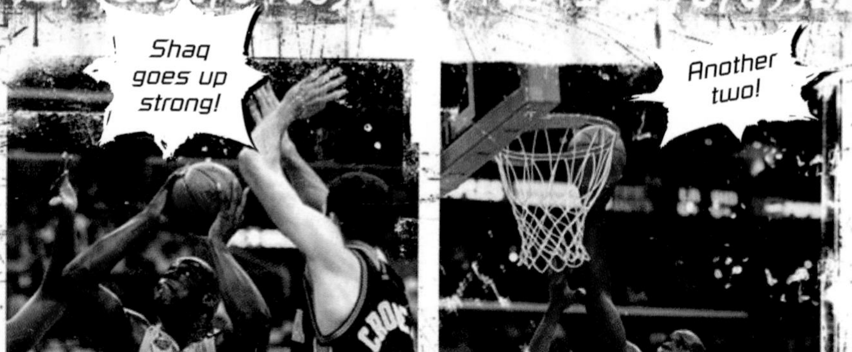
Shaq goes up strong!
ARGH!
Another two!

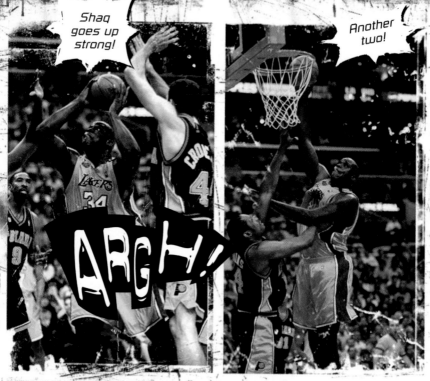

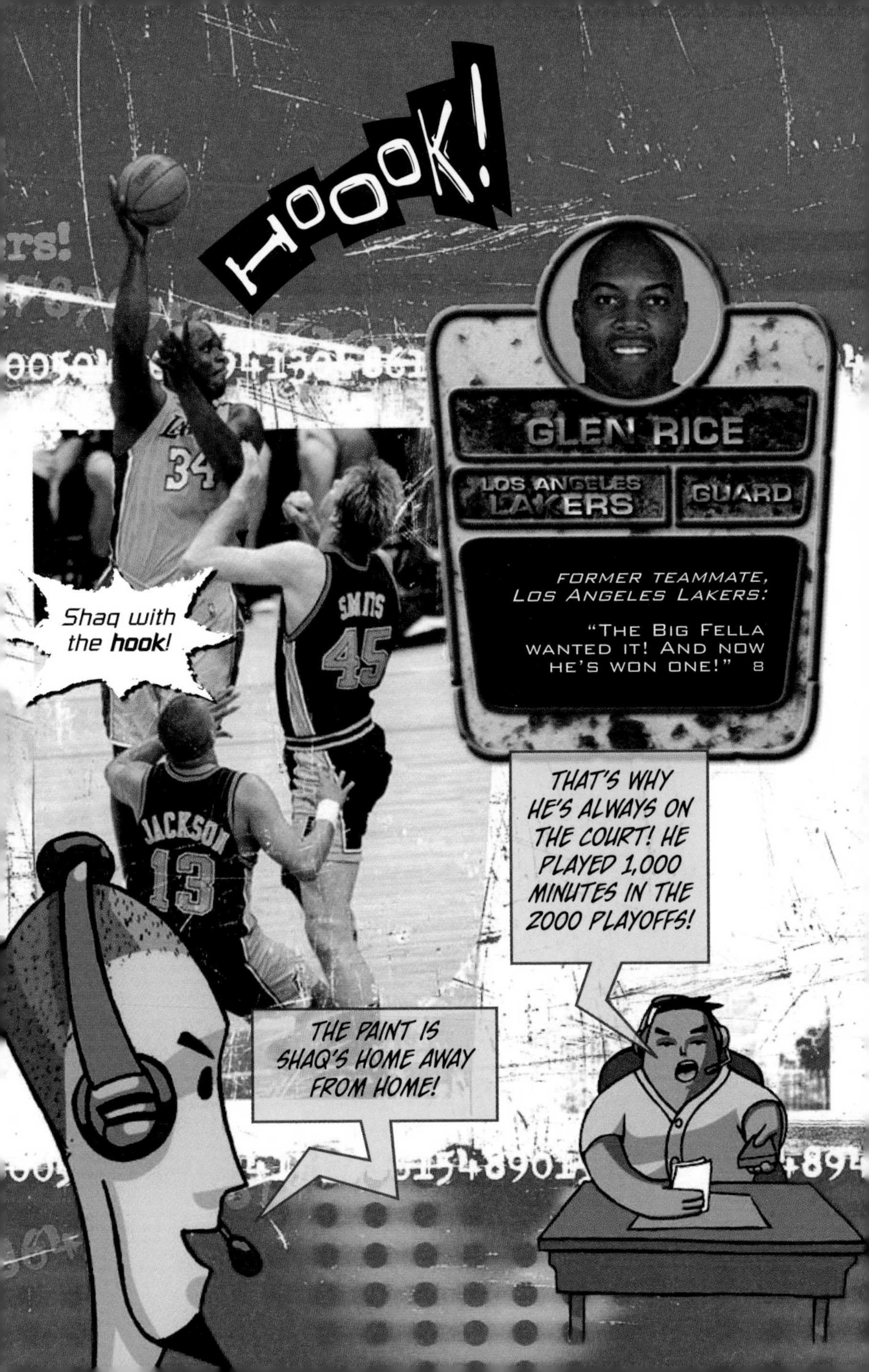
HOOOOK!
Shaq with the **hook**!
GLEN RICE
LOS ANGELES LAKERS
GUARD
FORMER TEAMMATE, LOS ANGELES LAKERS:
"THE BIG FELLA WANTED IT! AND NOW HE'S WON ONE!" 8
THAT'S WHY HE'S ALWAYS ON THE COURT! HE PLAYED 1,000 MINUTES IN THE 2000 PLAYOFFS!
THE PAINT IS SHAQ'S HOME AWAY FROM HOME!

June 2000:
First Championship (vs. Pacers)!

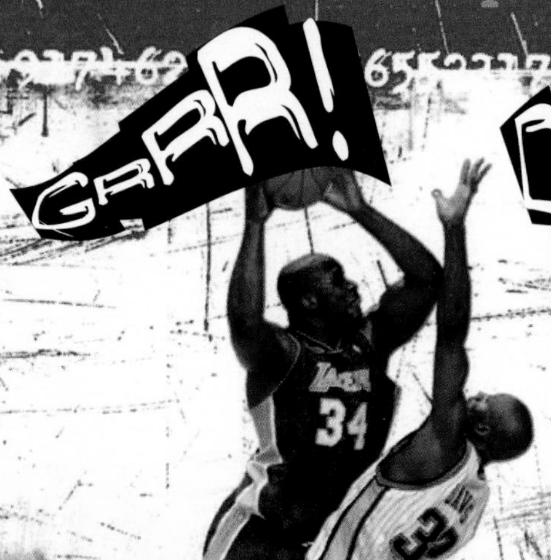
GRRR!

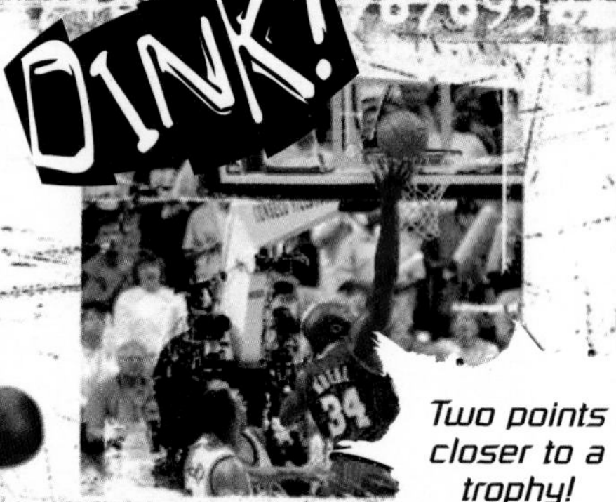
DINK!
Two points closer to a trophy!

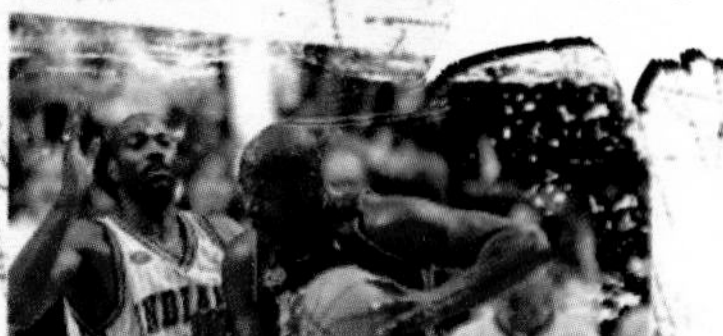
SWOOP!
To the hole!

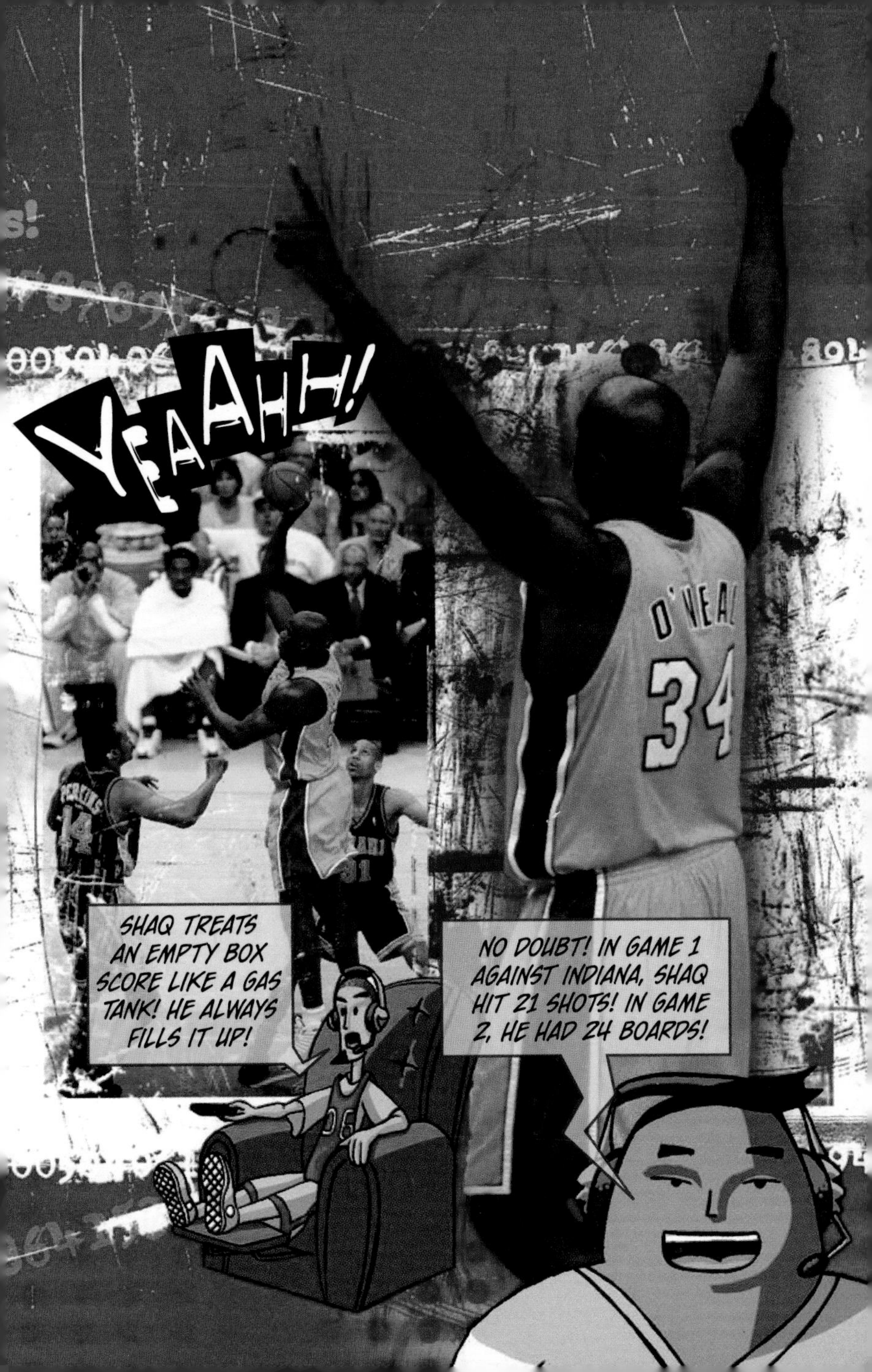
YEAAHH!
O'NEAL
34
SHAQ TREATS AN EMPTY BOX SCORE LIKE A GAS TANK! HE ALWAYS FILLS IT UP!
NO DOUBT! IN GAME 1 AGAINST INDIANA, SHAQ HIT 21 SHOTS! IN GAME 2, HE HAD 24 BOARDS!

June 2000:
First Title Celebration!

They did it!
And it sure
wasn't easy!

BOO-YA!

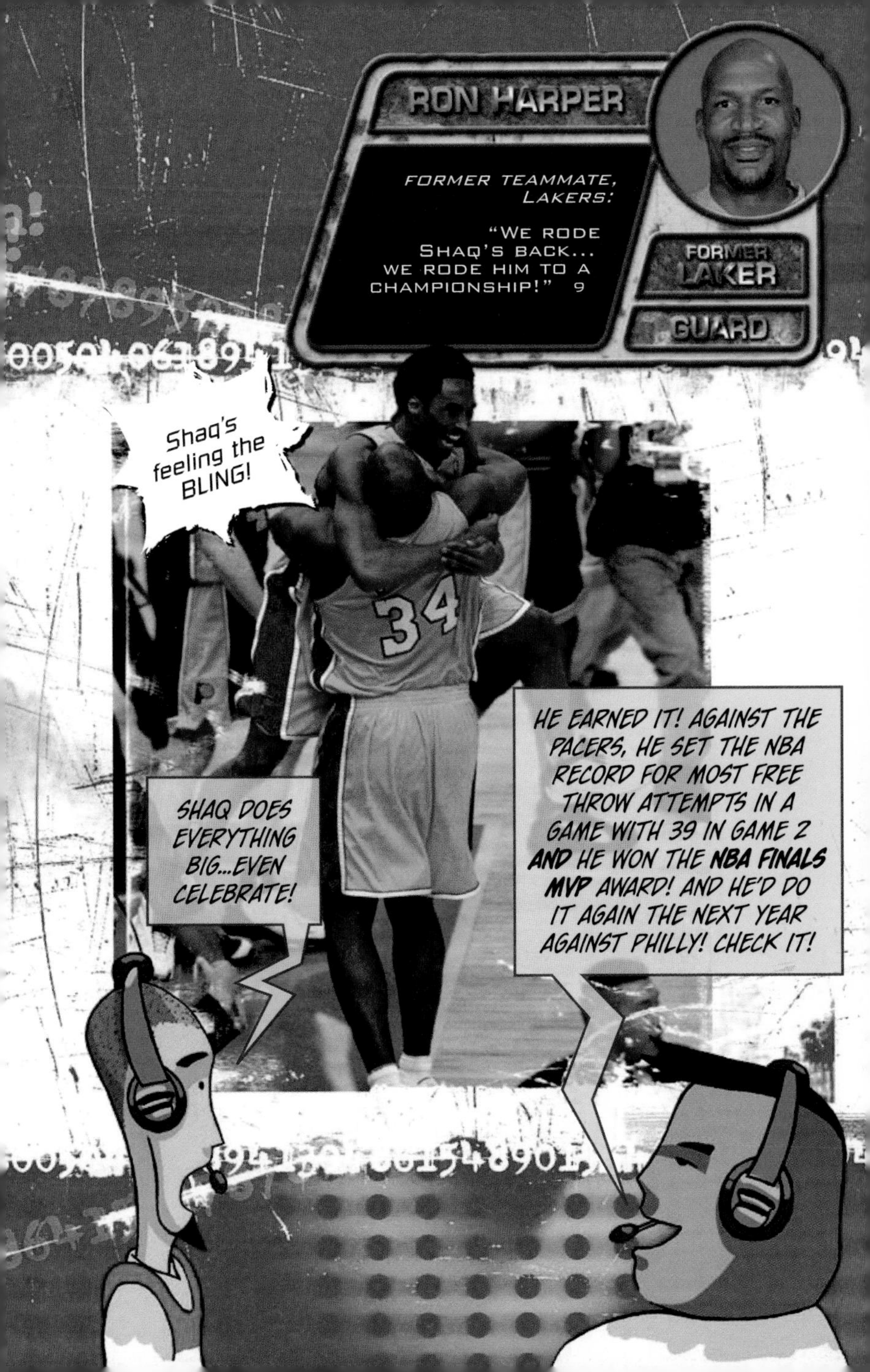
RON HARPER
FORMER TEAMMATE, LAKERS:
"WE RODE SHAQ'S BACK... WE RODE HIM TO A CHAMPIONSHIP!" 9
FORMER LAKER
GUARD
Shaq's feeling the BLING!
SHAQ DOES EVERYTHING BIG...EVEN CELEBRATE!
HE EARNED IT! AGAINST THE PACERS, HE SET THE NBA RECORD FOR MOST FREE THROW ATTEMPTS IN A GAME WITH 39 IN GAME 2 AND HE WON THE NBA FINALS MVP AWARD! AND HE'D DO IT AGAIN THE NEXT YEAR AGAINST PHILLY! CHECK IT!

June 2001: Trophy Number Two (vs. Philly)!

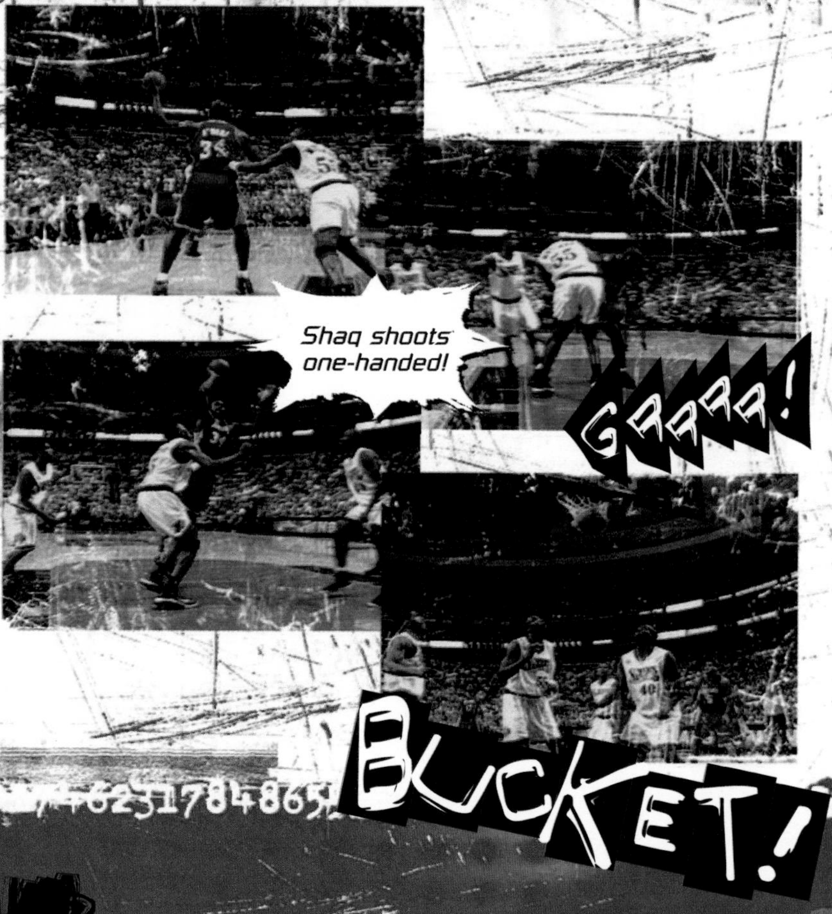
Shaq shoots one-handed!
GRRRR!
BUCKET!

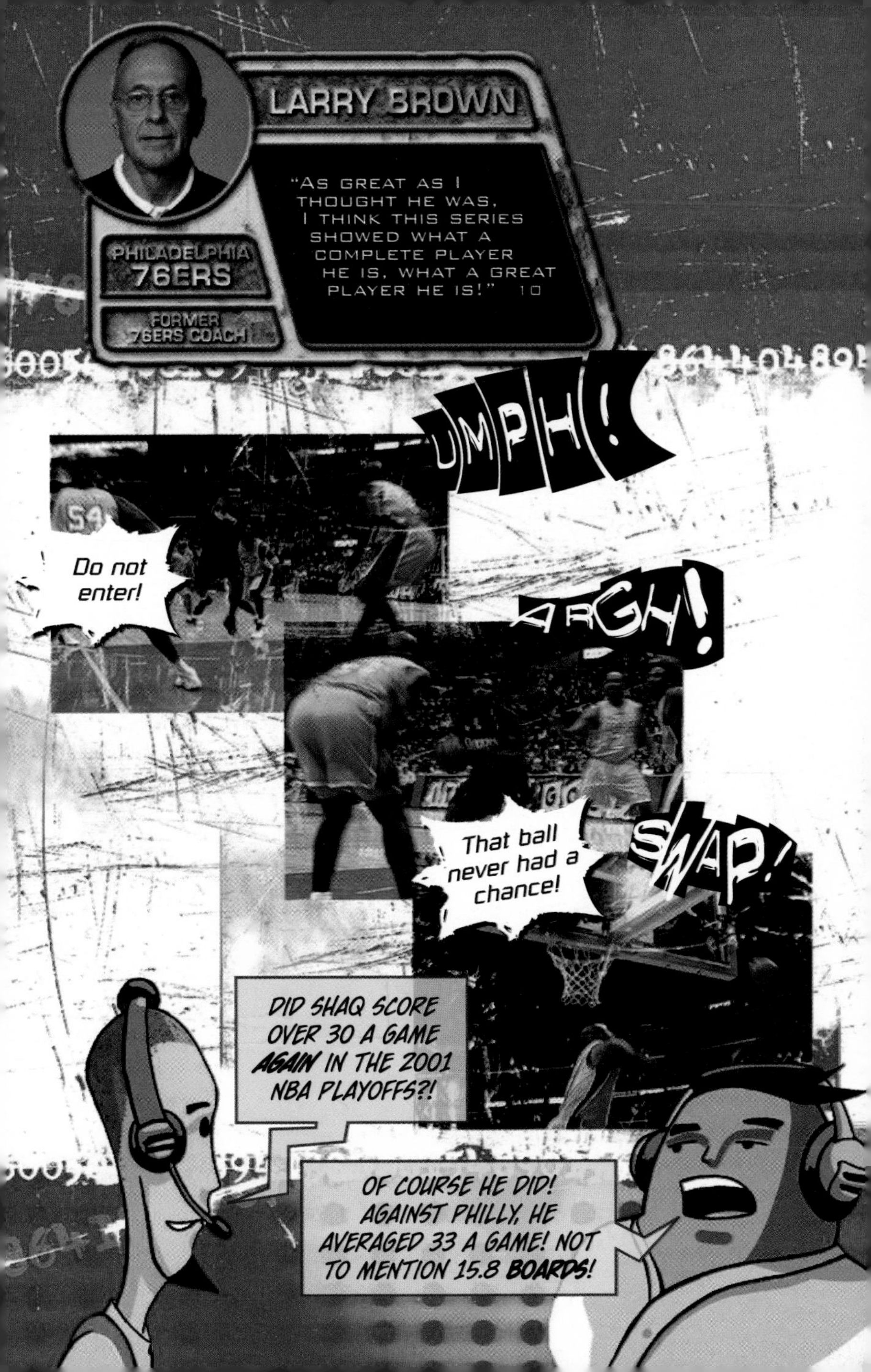
LARRY BROWN
PHILADELPHIA 76ERS
FORMER 76ERS COACH
"AS GREAT AS I THOUGHT HE WAS, I THINK THIS SERIES SHOWED WHAT A COMPLETE PLAYER HE IS, WHAT A GREAT PLAYER HE IS!" [10]
UMPH!
Do not enter!
ARGH!
That ball never had a chance!
SNAP!
DID SHAQ SCORE OVER 30 A GAME AGAIN IN THE 2001 NBA PLAYOFFS?!
OF COURSE HE DID! AGAINST PHILLY, HE AVERAGED 33 A GAME! NOT TO MENTION 15.8 BOARDS!

championship moments

June 2001: Trophy Number Two (vs. Philly)!

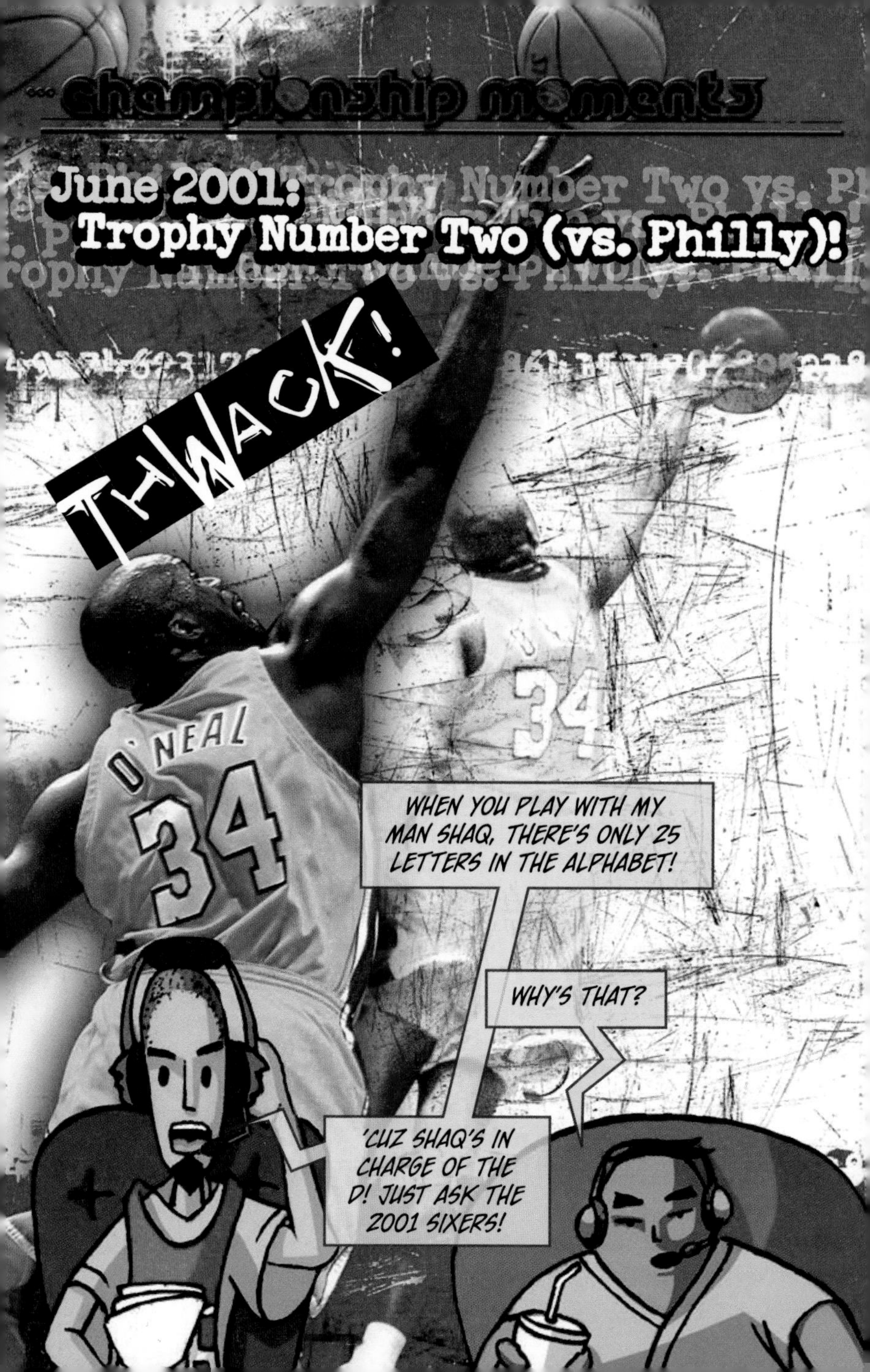
THWACK!
O'NEAL
34
34
WHEN YOU PLAY WITH MY MAN SHAQ, THERE'S ONLY 25 LETTERS IN THE ALPHABET!
WHY'S THAT?
'CUZ SHAQ'S IN CHARGE OF THE D! JUST ASK THE 2001 SIXERS!

TODD MACCULLOCH

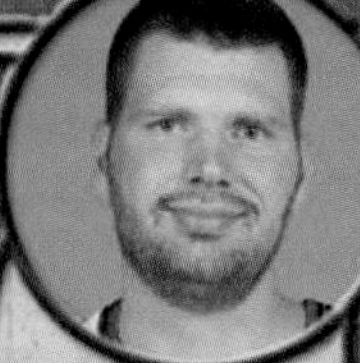

"Not only did he block the ball, but he kept it in bounds, and that led to their fast break!" 11

PHILADELPHIA 76ERS

CENTER

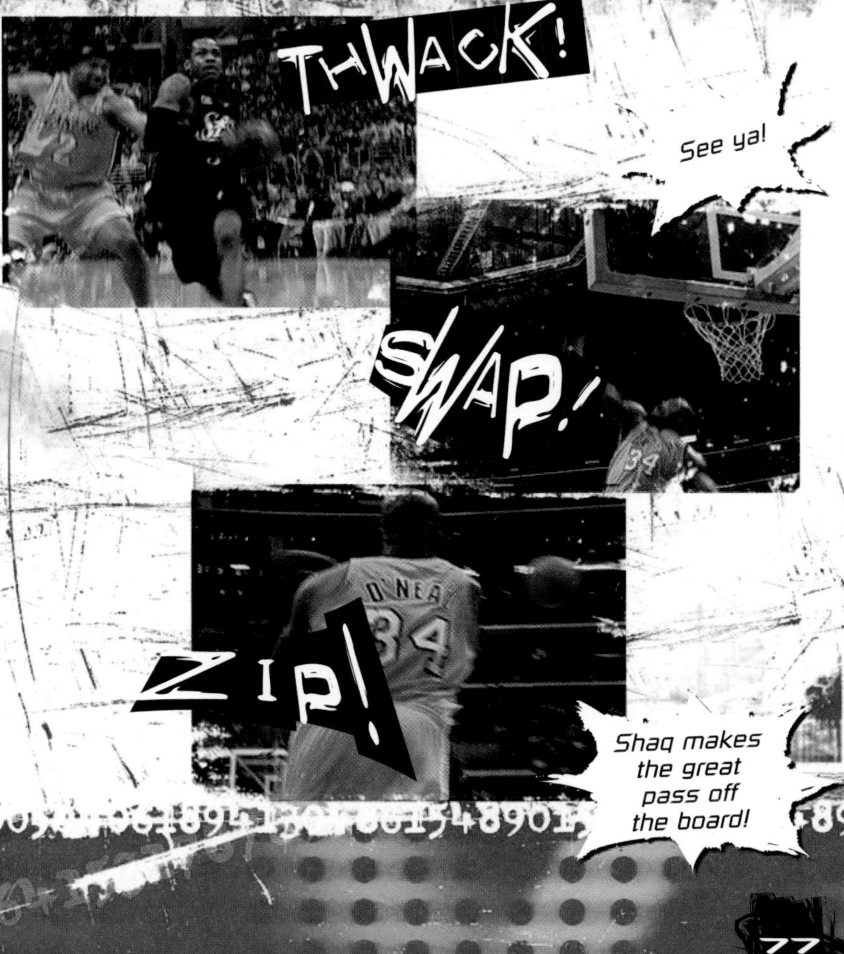

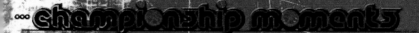

...championship moments

June 2001: Trophy Number Two (vs. Philly)!

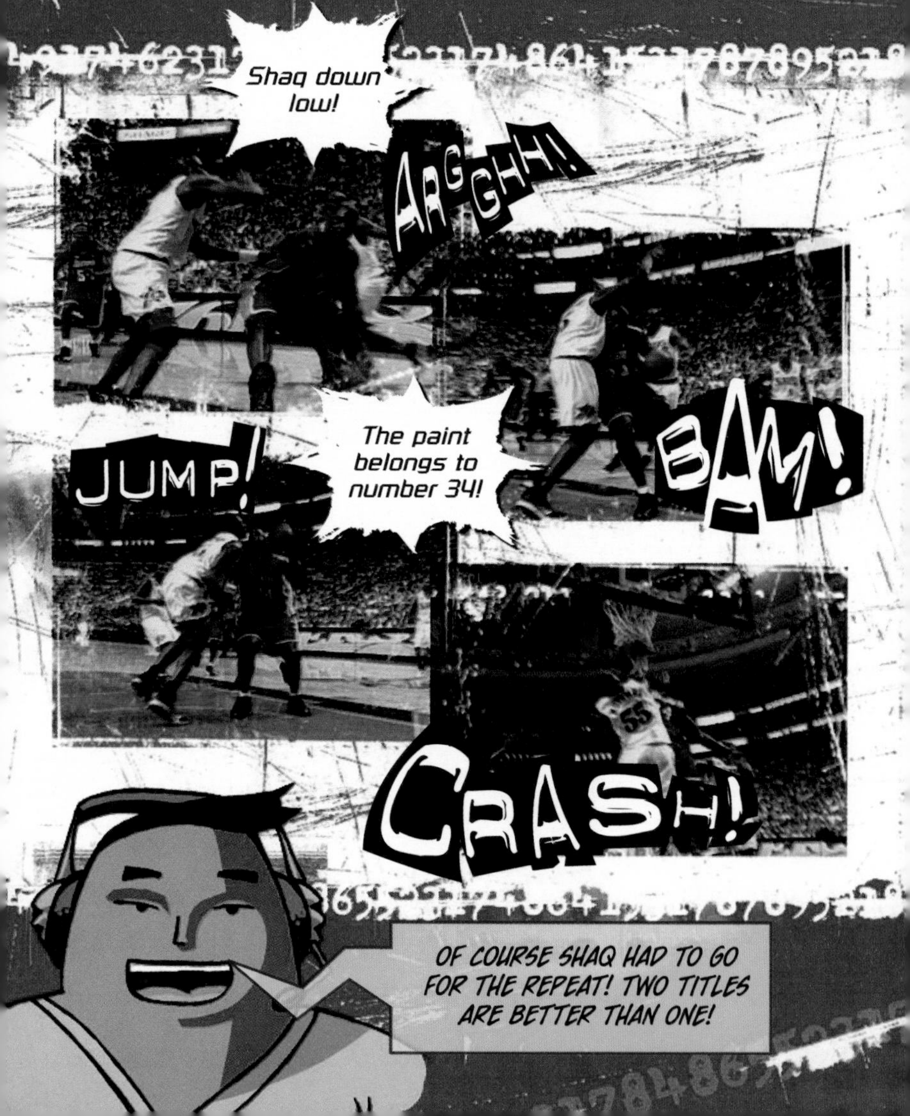
Shaq down low!
ARGGHH!
JUMP!
The paint belongs to number 34!
BAM!
CRASH!
OF COURSE SHAQ HAD TO GO FOR THE REPEAT! TWO TITLES ARE BETTER THAN ONE!

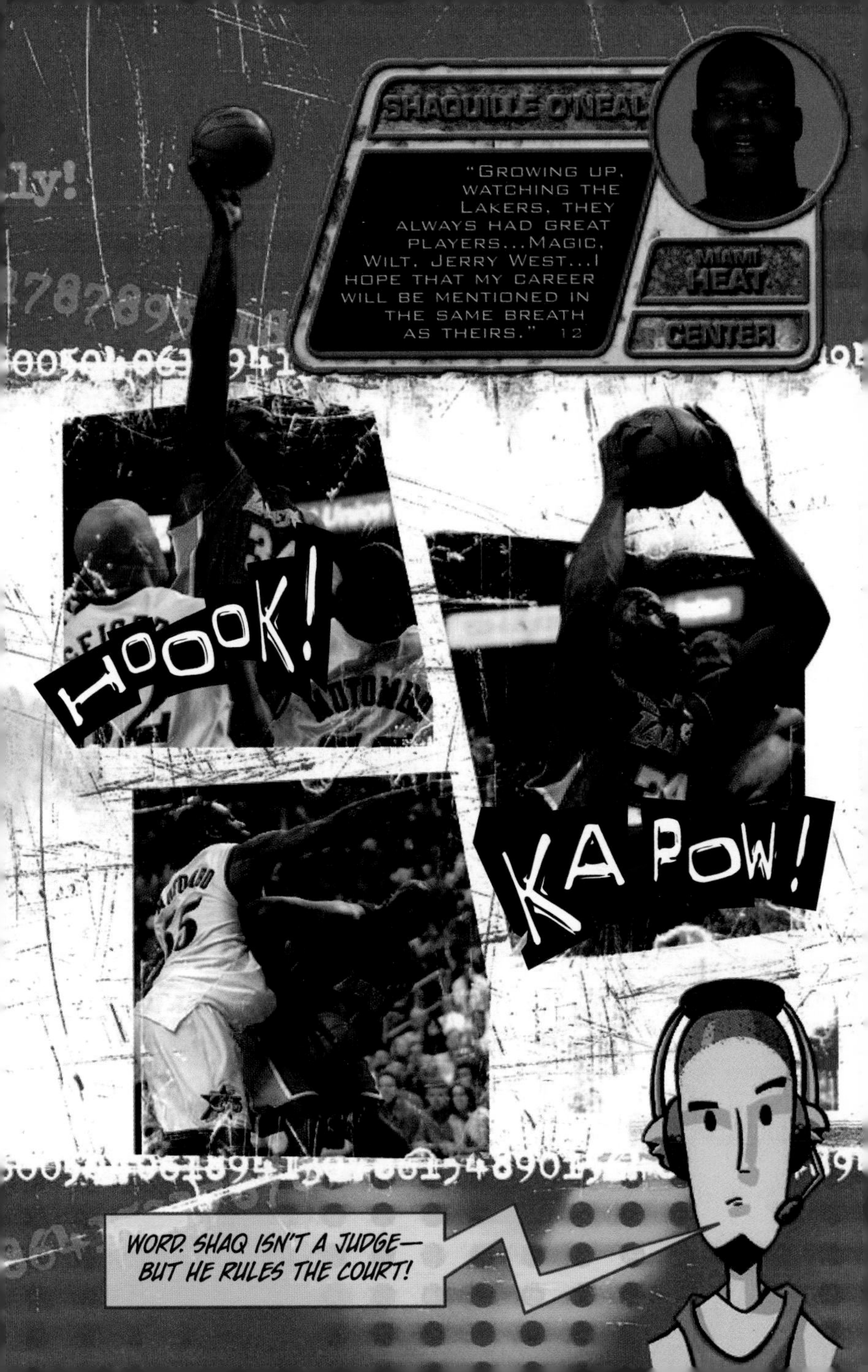
SHAQUILLE O'NEAL
"GROWING UP, WATCHING THE LAKERS, THEY ALWAYS HAD GREAT PLAYERS...MAGIC, WILT, JERRY WEST...I HOPE THAT MY CAREER WILL BE MENTIONED IN THE SAME BREATH AS THEIRS." 12
MIAMI HEAT
CENTER
HOOOK!
KAPOW!
WORD. SHAQ ISN'T A JUDGE—BUT HE RULES THE COURT!

June 2002: Trophy Three (vs. New Jersey)!

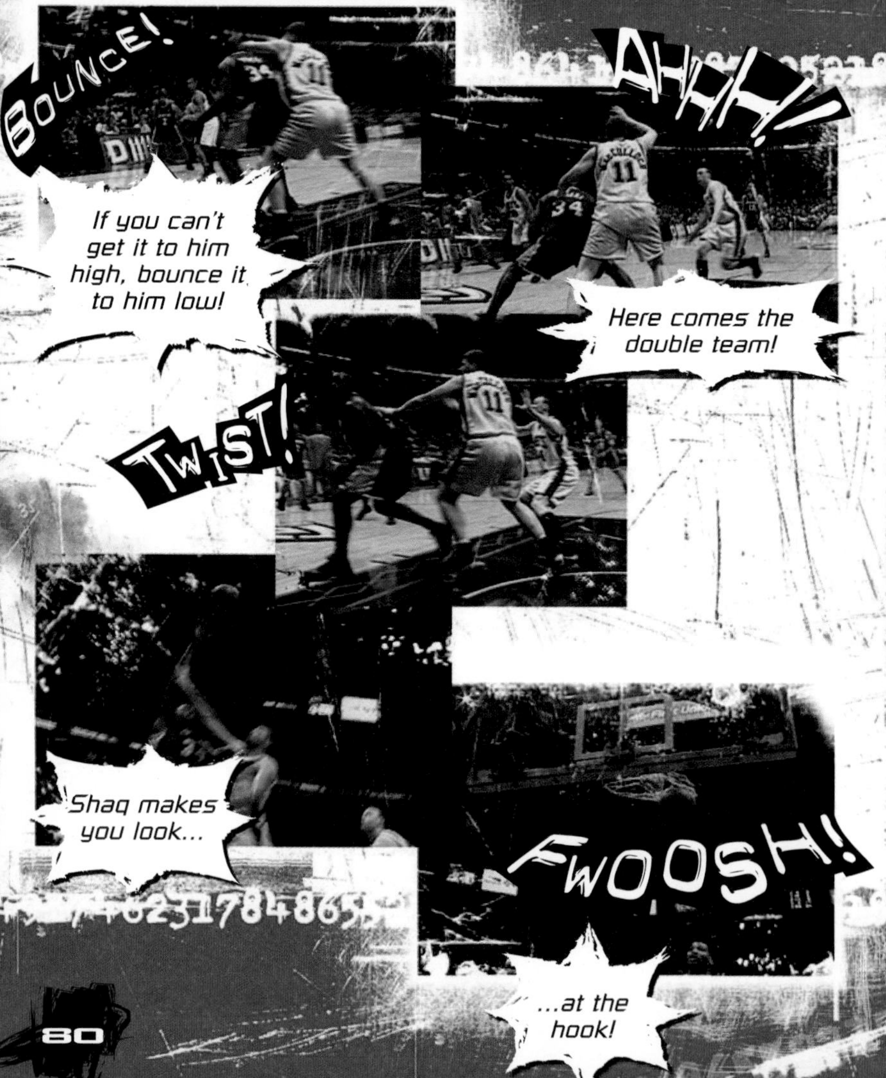

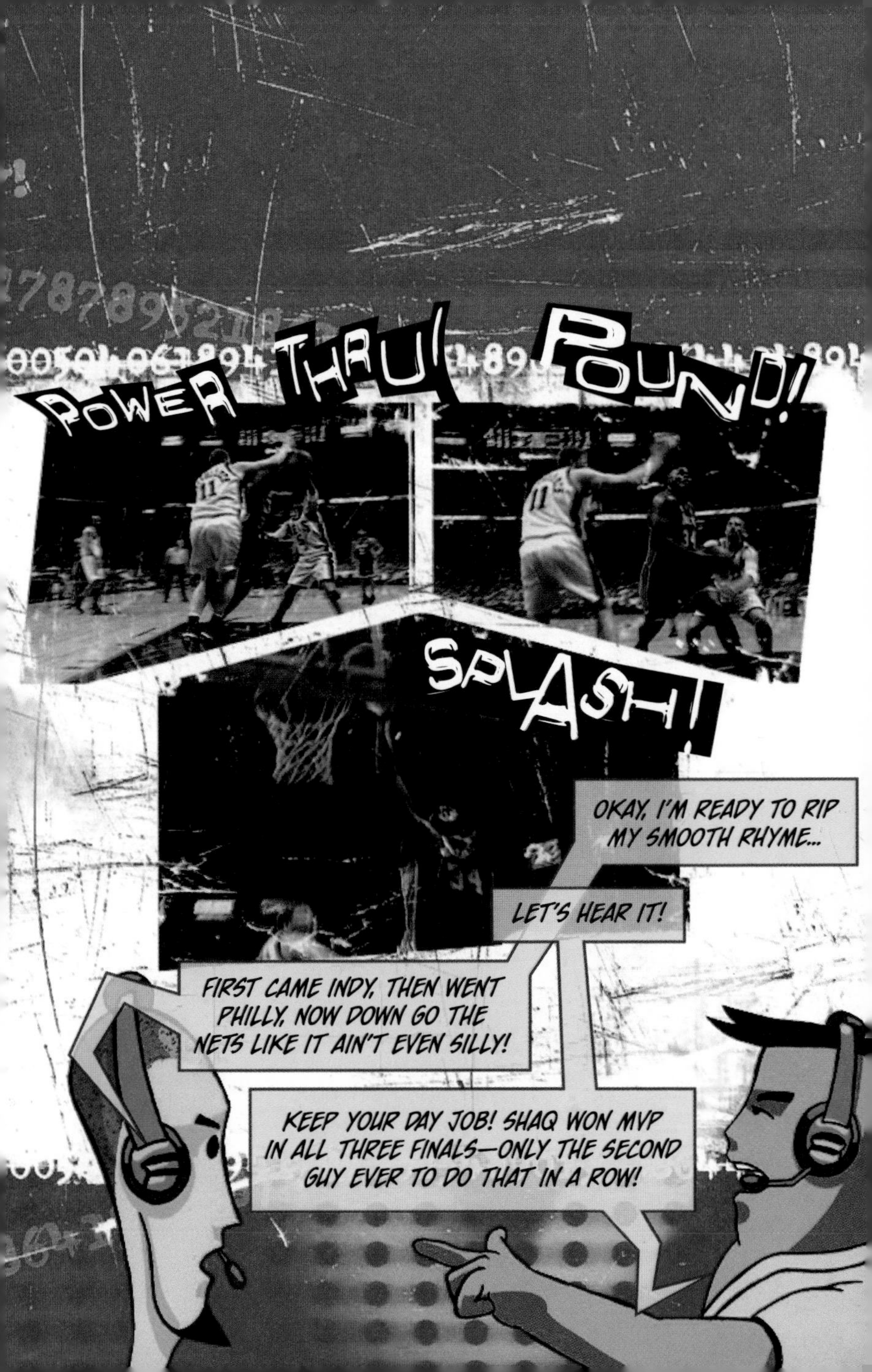
POWER THRU!
POUND!
SPLASH!
OKAY, I'M READY TO RIP MY SMOOTH RHYME...
LET'S HEAR IT!
FIRST CAME INDY, THEN WENT PHILLY, NOW DOWN GO THE NETS LIKE IT AIN'T EVEN SILLY!
KEEP YOUR DAY JOB! SHAQ WON MVP IN ALL THREE FINALS—ONLY THE SECOND GUY EVER TO DO THAT IN A ROW!

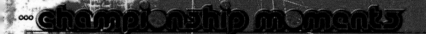

...championship moments

June 2002: Trophy Three (vs. New Jersey)!

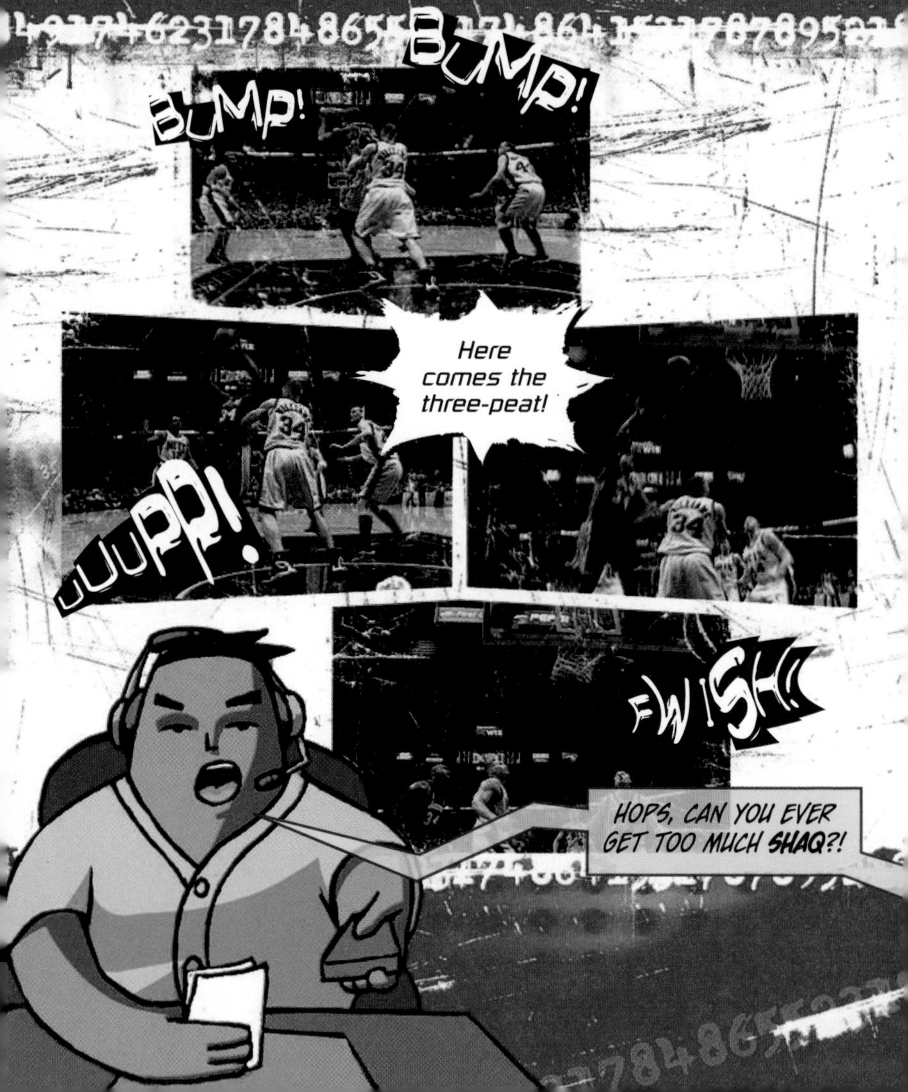
BUMP!
BUMP!
Here comes the three-peat!
UUUPP!
FWISH!
HOPS, CAN YOU EVER GET TOO MUCH SHAQ?!

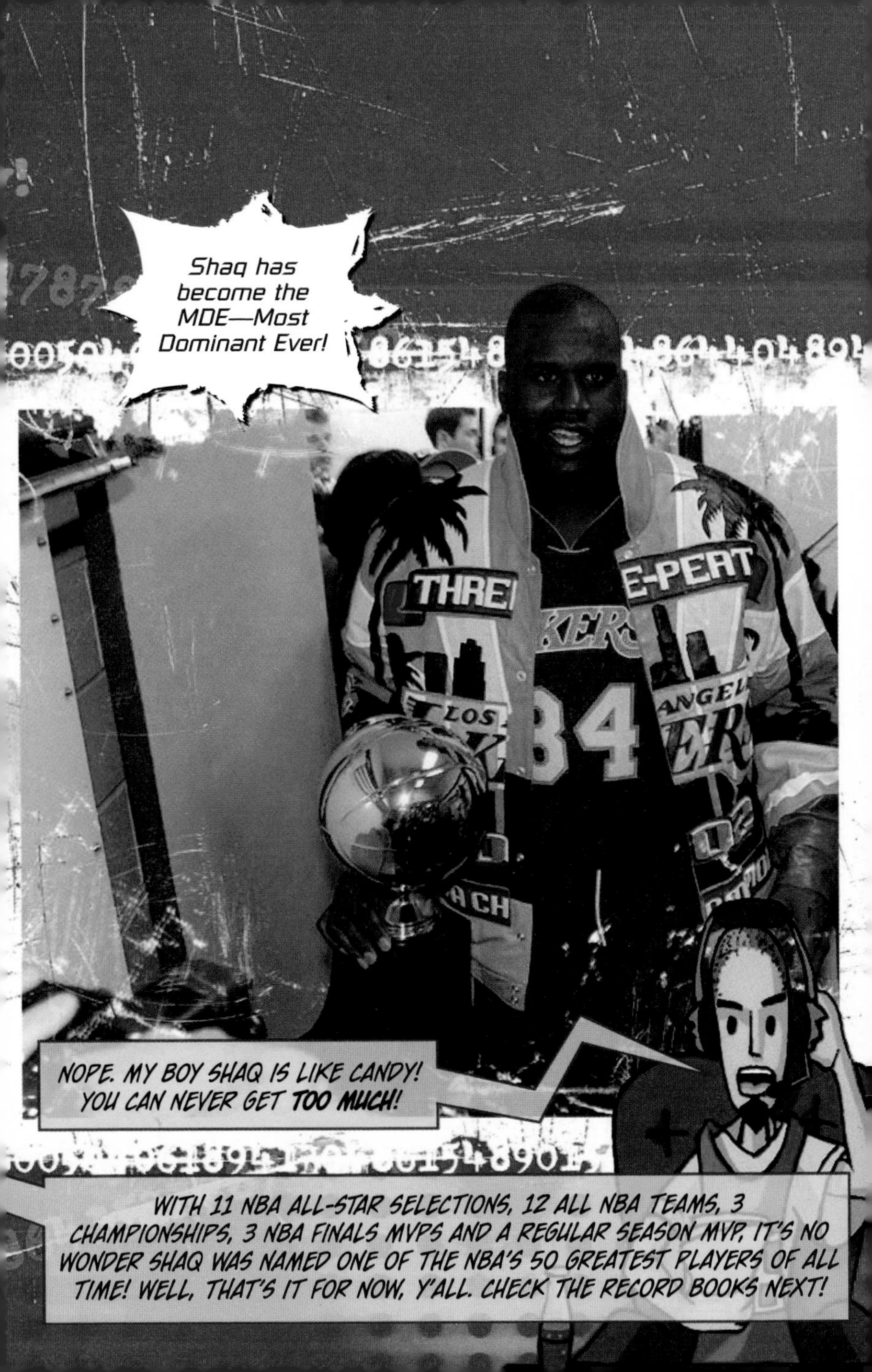

Shaq has become the MDE—Most Dominant Ever!
THREE-PEAT
NOPE. MY BOY SHAQ IS LIKE CANDY! YOU CAN NEVER GET **TOO MUCH!**
WITH 11 NBA ALL-STAR SELECTIONS, 12 ALL NBA TEAMS, 3 CHAMPIONSHIPS, 3 NBA FINALS MVPS AND A REGULAR SEASON MVP, IT'S NO WONDER SHAQ WAS NAMED ONE OF THE NBA'S 50 GREATEST PLAYERS OF ALL TIME! WELL, THAT'S IT FOR NOW, Y'ALL. CHECK THE RECORD BOOKS NEXT!

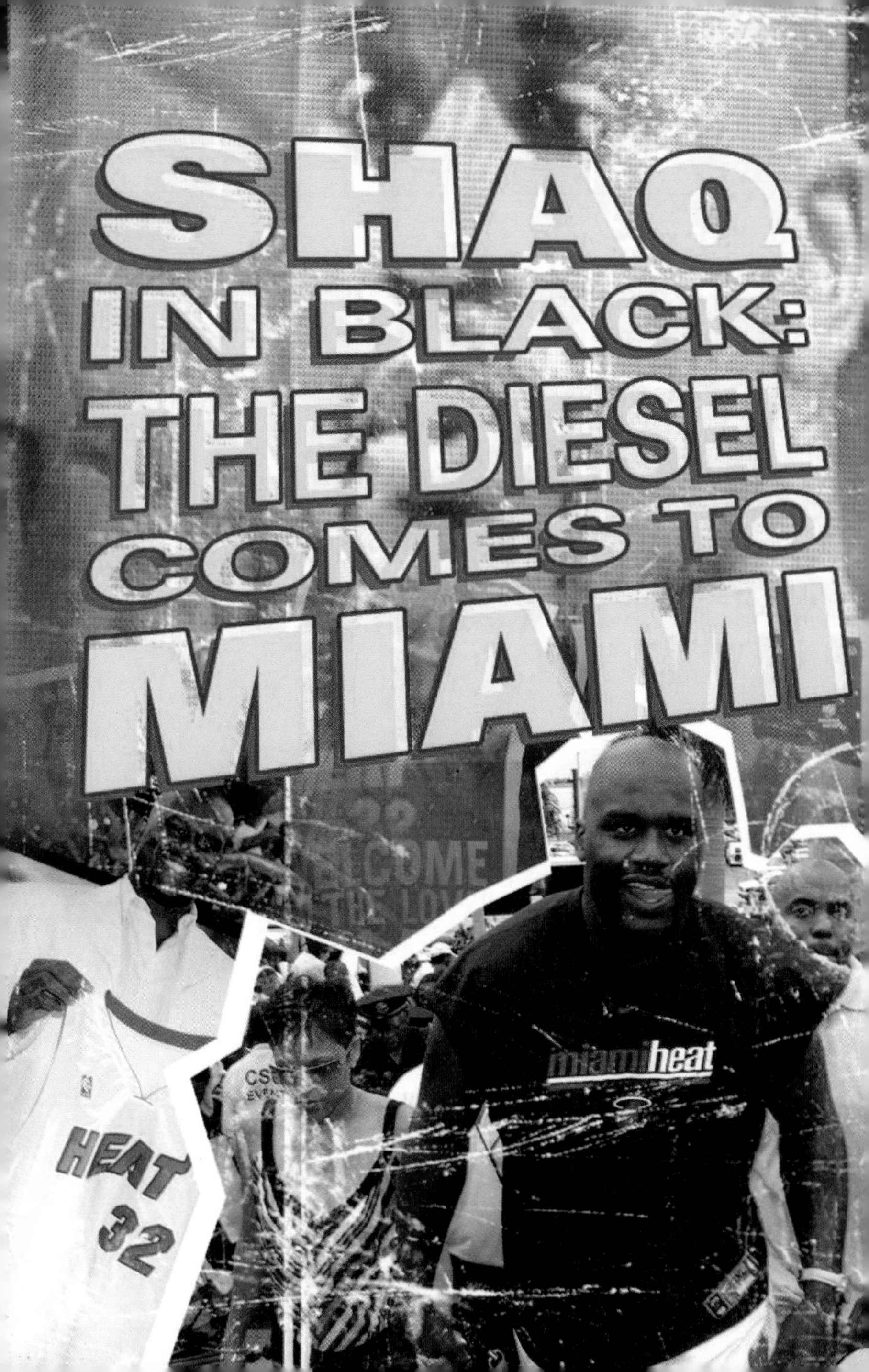
SHAQ
IN BLACK:
THE DIESEL
COMES TO
MIAMI
HEAT
32
miamiheat

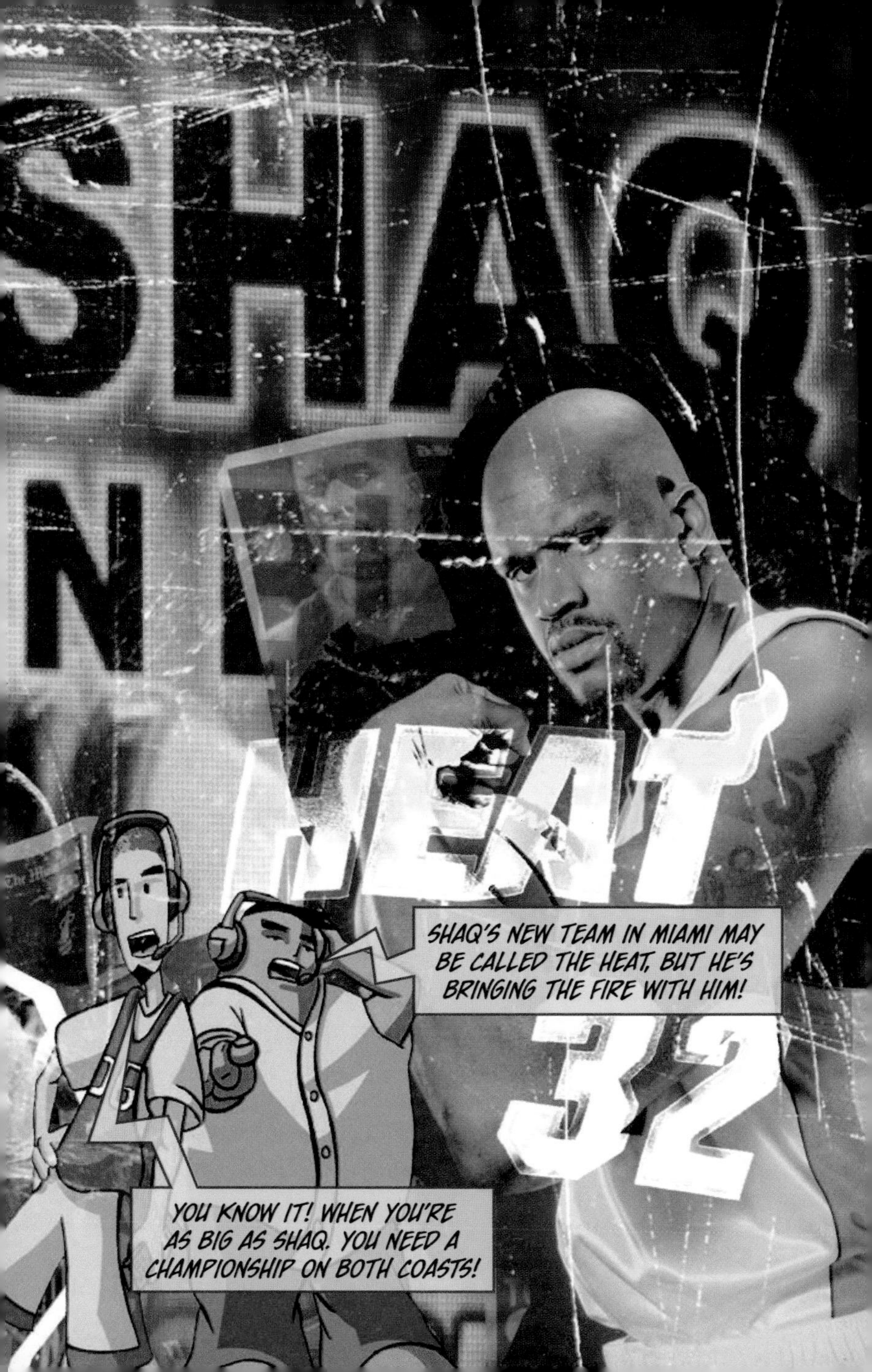
SHAQ'S NEW TEAM IN MIAMI MAY BE CALLED THE HEAT, BUT HE'S BRINGING THE FIRE WITH HIM!
YOU KNOW IT! WHEN YOU'RE AS BIG AS SHAQ. YOU NEED A CHAMPIONSHIP ON BOTH COASTS!

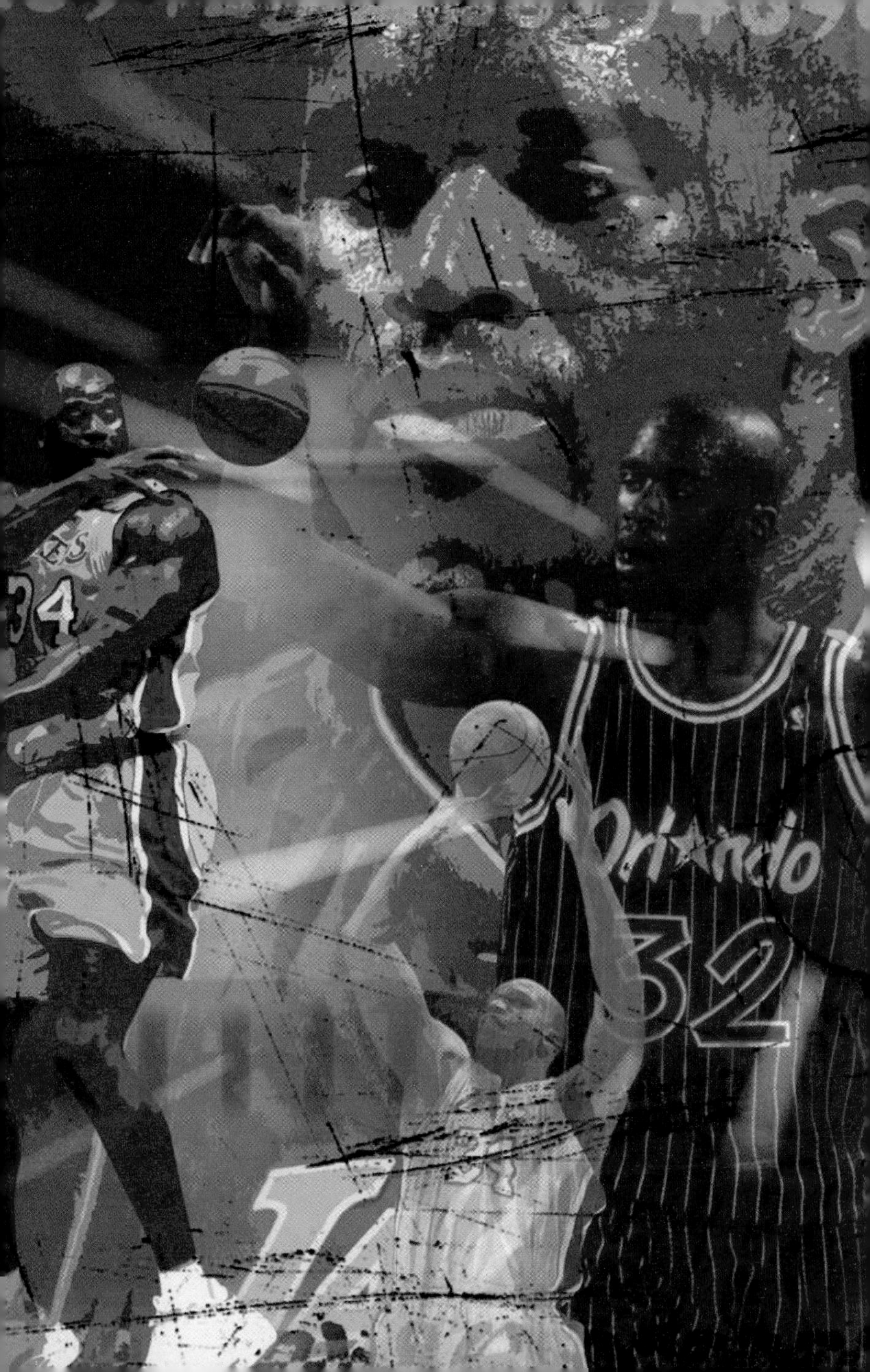
32

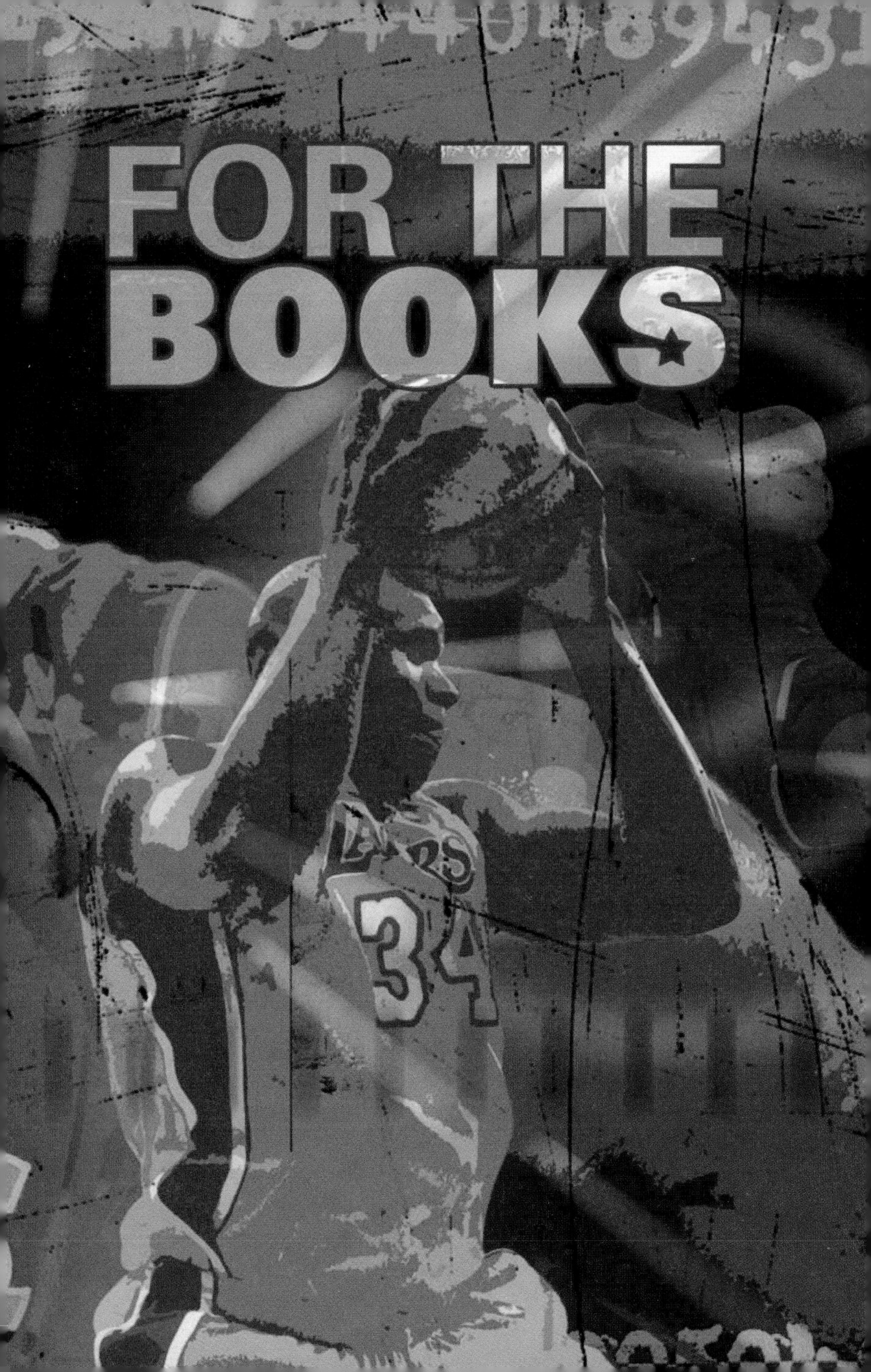

FOR THE
BOOKS
34

TIMELINE

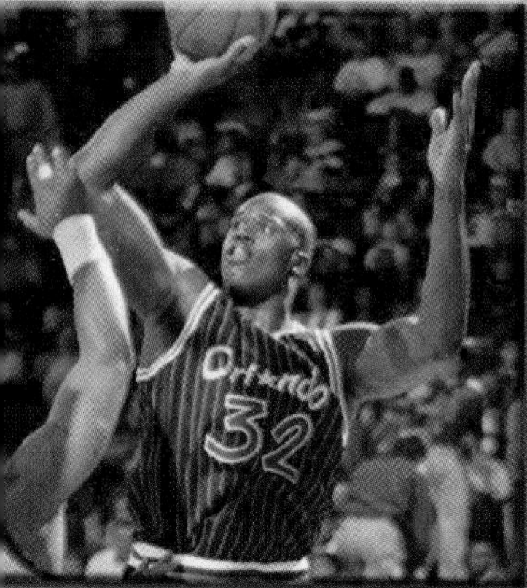
Orlando
32

1991 Shaq named College Basketball Player of the Year as a junior by AP and *Sports Illustrated*.

1992 Drafted #1 overall in the NBA Draft by the Orlando Magic.

1993 First player in NBA history to be named Player of the Week in his first week.

1994 Averaged 23.4 points, 13.9 boards in his first NBA season. Earned NBA Rookie of the Year Award. Played in first NBA playoff series.

1995 Led the NBA in scoring with 29.3 points per game. Won Eastern Conference Championship with Magic.

1996 Led the Magic in points (26.6), rebounds (11) and blocked shots (2.13) per game. Signed as a free agent with the Lakers.

1997 Named Third Team All-NBA. Only player in NBA that year to average 25 points and 10 boards.

1998 Led the NBA in field goal percentage (.584). Scored the 10,000th point of his career on February 10. First Laker since Magic Johnson to score 30 points in 4 consecutive games.

1999 Averaged 26.6 points and 11.6 boards a game in the playoffs.

2000 Finished season first in scoring (29.7), second in rebounds (13.6) and third in blocked shots (3.04). Won Regular Season MVP Award, All-Star Game MVP Award and Finals MVP Award. Named First Team All-NBA. Selected to the Second Team All-Defense. Won first NBA title.

2001 Named starting center for All-Star team for third consecutive season. Became 85th player in NBA history to tally 15,000 points. Averaged 33.3 points and 17.3 rebounds in the Western Conference Finals vs. Spurs. Won Second NBA Title.

2002 Named Western Conference Player of the Week three times. Registered 40 double-doubles. Named NBA Finals MVP and won third NBA Title.

2003 Recorded his 9,000th career rebound on April 15. Moved into sixth position All-Time in Playoff Points with 3,821. Post-season scoring average (28.1) ranked fourth All-Time.

2004 Ranked first in NBA in Free Throw Attempts (676) and field goal percentage (.584). Averaged at least 20 points and 10 boards a game for the 12th consecutive season. Acquired by Miami Heat in a trade with Lakers during summer.

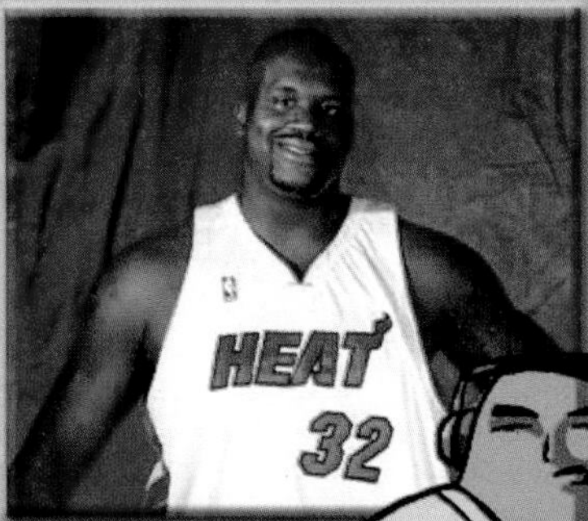
HEAT
32

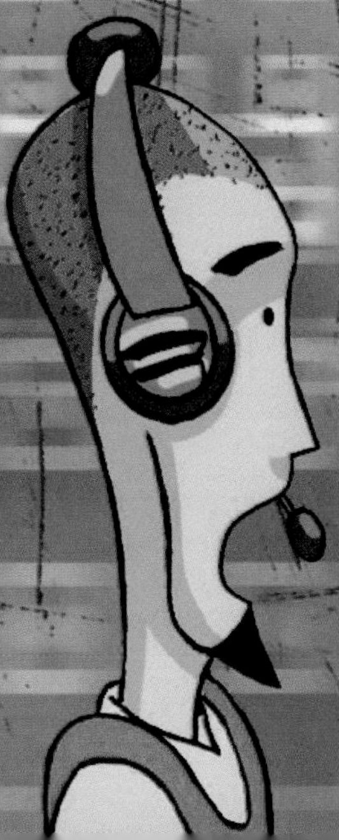

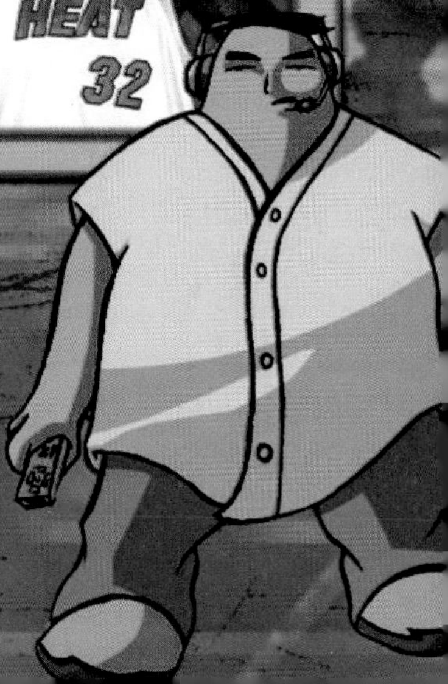

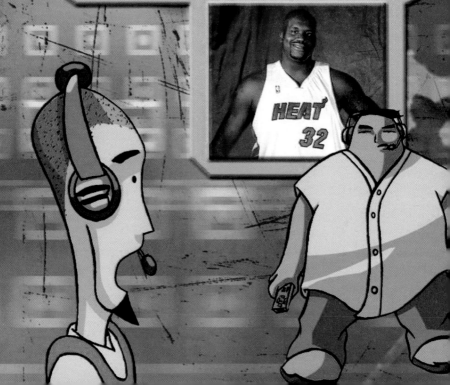

SHAQ INDEX:
COOL STATS AND FACTS

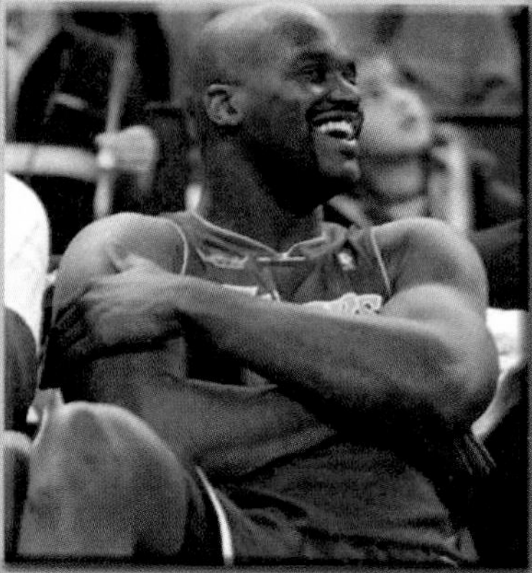

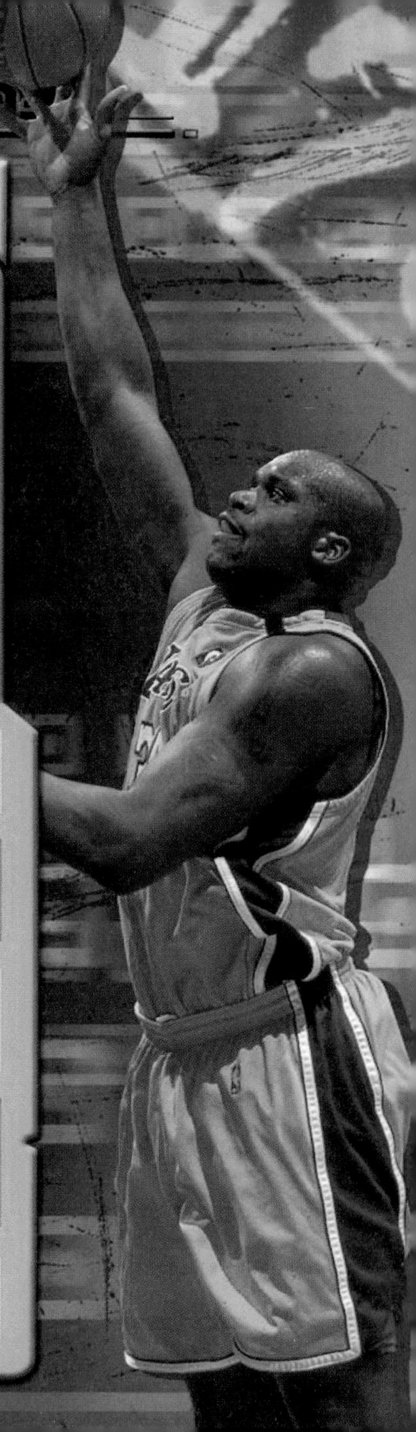

Number of times Shaq has earned All-NBA honors: **12**

The only two legends Shaq's career scoring average is behind: **Michael Jordan and Wilt Chamberlain**

The event in which Shaq has the second highest All-Time career scoring average: **NBA Finals (34.2)**

First player since Kareem Abdul-Jabbar in '76-'77 to do this: **rank top three in PPG, rebounds, field goal percentage and blocked shots in one season (1999-2000)**

Number of albums Shaq's debut cut, *Shaq Diesel*, sold: **over one million**

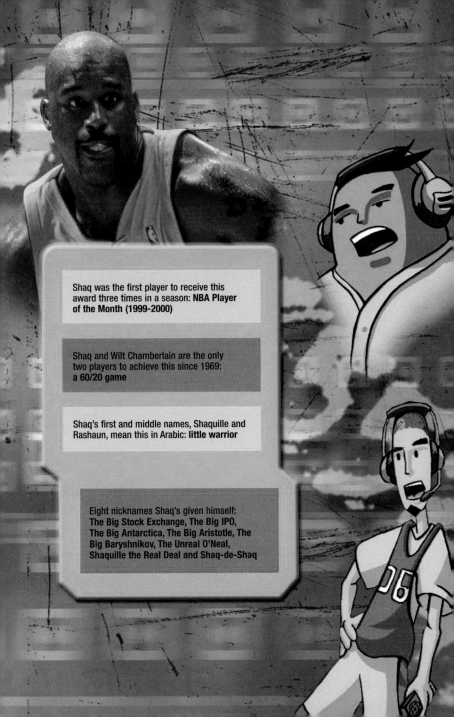

Shaq was the first player to receive this award three times in a season: **NBA Player of the Month (1999-2000)**

Shaq and Wilt Chamberlain are the only two players to achieve this since 1969: **a 60/20 game**

Shaq's first and middle names, Shaquille and Rashaun, mean this in Arabic: **little warrior**

Eight nicknames Shaq's given himself: **The Big Stock Exchange, The Big IPO, The Big Antarctica, The Big Aristotle, The Big Baryshnikov, The Unreal O'Neal, Shaquille the Real Deal and Shaq-de-Shaq**

CAREER MILESTONES

Regular Season Highs

POINTS: 61 vs. L.A. Clippers, 3/6/00

REBOUNDS: 28 vs. New Jersey, 11/20/93

BLOCKS: 15 vs. New Jersey, 11/20/93

ASSISTS: 9 vs. Orlando, 2/18/00

Playoff Highs

POINTS: 46 vs. Sacramento, 4/23/00

REBOUNDS: 24 vs. Indiana, 6/9/00

BLOCKS: 8 vs. Philadelphia, 6/8/01

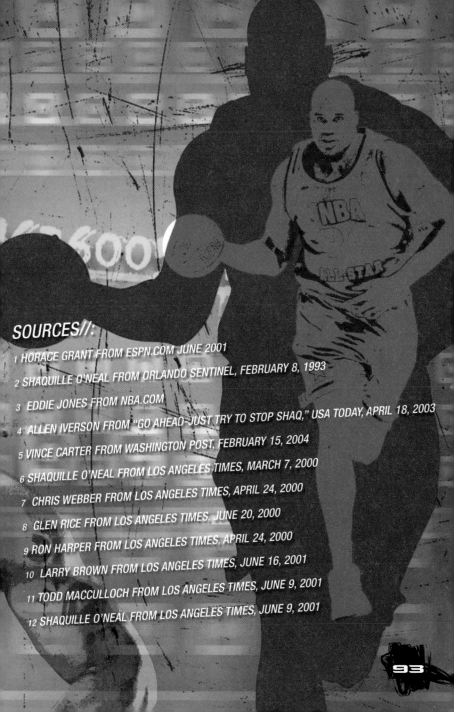

SOURCES//:

1 HORACE GRANT FROM ESPN.COM JUNE 2001

2 SHAQUILLE O'NEAL FROM ORLANDO SENTINEL, FEBRUARY 8, 1993

3 EDDIE JONES FROM NBA.COM

4 ALLEN IVERSON FROM "GO AHEAD-JUST TRY TO STOP SHAQ," USA TODAY, APRIL 18, 2003

5 VINCE CARTER FROM WASHINGTON POST, FEBRUARY 15, 2004

6 SHAQUILLE O'NEAL FROM LOS ANGELES TIMES, MARCH 7, 2000

7 CHRIS WEBBER FROM LOS ANGELES TIMES, APRIL 24, 2000

8 GLEN RICE FROM LOS ANGELES TIMES, JUNE 20, 2000

9 RON HARPER FROM LOS ANGELES TIMES, APRIL 24, 2000

10 LARRY BROWN FROM LOS ANGELES TIMES, JUNE 16, 2001

11 TODD MACCULLOCH FROM LOS ANGELES TIMES, JUNE 9, 2001

12 SHAQUILLE O'NEAL FROM LOS ANGELES TIMES, JUNE 9, 2001

ALSO AVAILABLE FROM TOKYOPOP

MANGA